Living Doctrine in a Vital Pulpit

MERRILL R. ABBEY

Living Doctrine in a
Vital
Pulpit

❦

Abingdon Press
new york
nashville

To Lucy

To Lucy

❧
Preface

The flow of traffic on the thoroughfare between doctrine and life situations gauges vitality in preaching. Sermons which confront human affairs as if they had no roots in doctrine shrink to cozy chats on small matters. Dealing in doctrine not newly challenged by the living human scene, they become arid. Holding the two elements together, preaching grows prophetic.

These chapters stand on this conviction. They continue an enterprise begun in *Preaching to the Contemporary Mind.* That study focused on men in their situations and sought to guide the preacher over the route of double analysis to biblical and doctrinal insight. Here we are no less concerned to relate human scene to spiritual resource. For purposes of clarity in consideration, we direct attention to traffic flowing in the opposite direction on the same highway.

7

Once the interpreter of the gospel has learned the elements of homiletic principle, he can progress best by relating his study of method to the problems and opportunities that inhere in specific aspects of the message. In a study of doctrinal preaching he ought to confront the central emphases in Christian teaching, wrestle with the task of formulating them into sermonic ideas, and preach them. For that reason, I have offered chapters on the several elements of the kerygma—foundation of the structure of Christian doctrine—with the intent not to tell the reader what and how to preach but to stimulate his creativity in approaching these cardinal concerns.

This study attempts to relate the central doctrinal core of the church's faith to the needs of a moving pulpit message by indicating how doctrines can be made clear and relevant to the lay mind, by appropriating the religious experiences great doctrines express, and by showing how their resources can be released to meet individual and social need. For that reason, it should be helpful to any thoughtful reader seeking a better understanding of the Christian faith or guidance to more effective witness.

It is primarily intended, however, for the preacher seeking help in planning his message over longer periods; the minister aware of the taxing demand of being at once evangelist, prophet, and teacher of the church; the messenger hungry for fresh stimulation of his creative thought; and the student embarking on the alluring though stormy seas of homiletic adventure. I offer it diffidently, since the task is momentous, but with confidence born of long testing these methods in the parish pulpit, followed by some years in classroom verification of their usefulness to others.

My indebtedness runs far beyond the horizons that a brief word of acknowledgment can sweep. Notes throughout the text point to immediate sources I can identify. These studies have been enriched by the lively company who have shared in them: ministers in pastors' schools and conferences in Pennsylvania, Ohio, Minnesota, and North Dakota; fellow workers in churches I have served; and a succession of students in my classes at Garrett Theological Seminary. I am deeply indebted to my colleague, Dr. Philip S. Watson, Harris Franklin Rall Professor of Systematic Theology, for his great kindness in reading the manuscript and sharing with me the benefits of his wisdom. His criticisms have led to the strengthening of the work at many points; for weaknesses that remain he must not, of course, be held responsible. I am grateful to my wife, who has cheerfully sacrificed vacation periods that this task might go forward, has done the arduous task of indexing, and has shared steadily in the study and concern it represents.

MERRILL R. ABBEY

Contents

11

Now God Has Shared Our Lot
He Holds Our World Together

Chapter 1

A Centered
Gospel for a World Off Center

Parable of the Doomed Flywheel

If H. L. Mencken's caustic figure, man a sick fly riding the giant flywheel of the cosmic universe, throws light anywhere, it is less on man himself than on his world. For in the power to create the figure lies its negation. No fly could ask such questions—What sort of being am I? Whence come? Bound whither? To what end?—as this metaphor purports to answer. But what if the human world we inhabit were the massive wheel its dizzy momentum intimates, the troubled vibrations of a violent age symptoms that now it runs off center?

One truth at least is clear: A flywheel working so will destroy itself. The laws of motion by which it operates have judged it. Inertia, gravity, momentum, forces centrifugal and

15

centripetal—factors whose freely given grace assured its use-fulness—now spell its doom. Only a restoration of the shaft to its true center can avail to save it. Short of that, to increase the power supply is to make more relentless the force that drives it to its fate. To accelerate its motion is to hasten the moment when it will fly apart. To reinforce it with material of greater tensile strength is to prolong the period of its eccentric operation but to render the final shattering no less sure.

Though man's affairs are not a wheel, and the analogy proves nothing about the life we share in a global society, the suggestive figure may serve to illuminate a meaning in the present hour. Hence a proposition: Given a world plight not unlike that of the flywheel running off center, a gospel which essays the momentous task of restoration must itself be truly centered in its proclamation. Four subpropositions help to probe this truth.

Saved by Recentering

First, a world off center cannot be saved short of recentering. Numerous symptoms betray our plight. Note one instance. Velocity increased beyond the speed of sound, far from saving, only makes more imminent the doom of an uncentered world now fifteen minutes from extinction.

To overlay our eccentric life with harder material, as we talk of "hardening our bases," does not rectify our plight. A spokesman for the sciences declares that answer futile. "We know, with the certainty of statistical truth," he says, "that if enough of these weapons are made—by enough different states—some of them are going to blow up. Through accident, or folly, or madness—but the motives don't matter. What does matter is the nature of the statistical fact." [1] So we flee from one failure to another. As with the wheel, increasing the mass only accentuates the problem; our swiftly multiplying population becomes a dangerous "explosion," the wealth of an affluent society a bone of contention.

Increasing applied power effects no cure. Successive ages discover again that power holds only such promise as another factor gives it. An ancient taunt, couched in terms of a mocking offer, makes this clear: "Come now, make a wager with my master the king of Assyria: I will give you two thousand horses, if you are able on your part to set riders upon them" (II Kings 18:23). In an age when the horse was the chief means of power for armies small by comparison with modern mass warfare, two thousand horses subtracted from one force and added to the other could make the decisive difference— save for one factor: Riders could not be found.

Now leap the centuries. A generation ago, before the advent of atomic energy, an economist and social thinker of some note reported that a survey of the world's power resources revealed a billion horsepower available to turn our wheels and do our work. They offered, he said, fabulous possibilities and unprecedented hazards. Summing up his case, he put it graphically: "From our brains have sprung a billion horses, now running wild and almost certain sooner or later to run amuck. Where are the riders with their whirling ropes; where the light-hearted youths to mount, be thrown, and rise to mount again?" [2] We have moved from a world power fund

---

[1] Quoted by O. Frederick Nolde in *God and the H-Bomb*, edited by Donald Keys (New York: Bellmeadows Press with Bernard Geis Associates, 1961), p. 196.

[2] Stuart Chase, *Waste and the Machine Age* (New York: League for Industrial Democracy, 1931), p. 62.

17

of a billion horsepower to such incalculable resources that we talk casually of megatons; yet now, as in the age of coal or horses, the hope of our energies resides in the ancient question: Can we set riders upon them?

All else failing, we have sought a corrective in the increasing sophistication of our machines. Automation has come. Two men now tend machines building a thousand radio sets a day, until recently the work of two hundred men. One man at a console of controls operates the pumps and tanks of an oil field of many acres. Machines transcribe dictation directly into type, so that soon a large office can run without stenographers. Machines are "taught" to make complex computations with lightning speed and to store reservoirs of information in their mechanical "memories." In many industries the programming of machines makes it possible for them to tend themselves. Far from removing the hazard, however, this presses with new poignancy the question many a man must ask: "Have I become superfluous? Is it true, as some have guessed, that man himself is obsolete?"

These symptoms of our loss of center recall the Bible's diagnosis. In Eden the serpent speaks our idiom: "You will not die. For God knows that when you eat of [the fruit of the tree] your eyes will be opened, and you will be like God, knowing good and evil" (Gen. 3:5). Knowing, that is, as God knows—with controlling, not obedient, knowledge. "Everything is relative," a popular axiom avers, thereby asserting independence of God's command, with freedom to act as circumstances make expedient. Is not man the measure of all things? Self-assertion—displacing the center of our life in a relation to God held true by obedient faith—hastens our destruction.

18

Needed: A Centered Gospel

See, then, a second proposition: To save a world off center, only a centered gospel can avail. It is fruitless to preach in such an age as if to lapsed Christians who can be set safely on their way again by what we have called "spiritual inspiration." Motivating and exhorting cannot suffice when men do not know the central truths of the gospel. Preaching as if we had only to refresh the vision of those who have temporarily forgotten does nothing to restore the lost center of an age which no longer believes—and does not believe because it does not know—the great realities of the Christian message. The urgent need now confronting us demands forthright preaching of basic Christian doctrine; for we preach to men who "have not lapsed from any faith, since they never had one. What they need is not chiding or exhortation, but sheer basic information." [3]

The behavior of churchmen tells the story. Note the widespread sense of inadequacy to explain the Christian faith displayed by parents puzzled by their children's questions. Men who have been willing to work hard on a church building committee grow suddenly embarrassed when asked to speak to a business associate about the personal meaning of their faith. Loyal church members repeat racist slogans, oblivious of the teaching that God has made of one blood all peoples and that the final judgment searches men in terms of what they have done to the least of Christ's brethren. Christians scramble to possess and exploit more and more of this world's goods, as if they had never been taught that God made the earth and it

[3] J. B. Phillips, *Good News* (New York: The Macmillan Company, 1963), p. 172.

is his. Men who can amiably tolerate blatant blasphemies against God and the sanctity of such holy institutions as marriage, turn harshly intolerant of those who question the war system and the equating of security with armed might, as if they had never learned a faith which teaches that God—who alone is ultimate power—is love, and he who dwells in love dwells in God. Considering themselves good Christians, men repeat the platitude that "all religions amount to the same thing in the end," unaware of their faith's claim to uniqueness in the good news that in Christ God visited our earth, gave himself on a Cross, died, and rose again to reconcile all men to himself.

The word "faith" itself has come to carry a depreciated meaning to which cartoonists shrewdly point. Eavesdrop for a moment on the conversation of two of Jules Feiffer's ironic characters. "I don't get aroused any more," complains one of them. Whereupon the other, in successive panels, ejaculates a series of horrendous terms calculated to arouse the most lethargic. "Missile madness!" he shouts. "Atomic holocaust! Brinksmanship! Rocket diplomacy! India! Berlin!" When the whole recital leaves his companion unmoved, he asks, "Do you think we've turned apathetic?" "Apathy is such a *bad* word," the other protests. "I'd hate to think it's apathy we suffer from. Let's just call it faith." [4] Once a complete commitment to a gospel sharply etched in particular teachings that challenged the secular world, faith has sunk to that level! A tranquilizer which, if distinguished from apathy in some subtle way, at least manifests to the outside observer a confusing likeness.

[4] See cartoon in *Christian Faith and the Contemporary Arts*, ed. Finley Eversole (Nashville: Abingdon Press, 1962), p. 224.

No preaching that consists of exhortation, "spiritual refreshment," and playing on men's attitudes will meet the need for a restored center. Only a profoundly theological gospel will do. It has always been basic doctrines that have moved men. T. R. Glover observed: "Four words destroyed slavery, 'For whom Christ died.'" These words, which have defeated more than one entrenched evil, constitute, as Halford E. Luccock remarked, one of the most theological of affirmations: "There is no power in the foggy idea that Jesus was a sympathetic person who sent his good wishes to everybody. Nor is there power to destroy evil in a general fog of sentimentality." But men attempt just that when they indulge such innocuous hopes as the one inscribed on the entrance to an outdoor theater in Cold Water Canyon at Beverly Hills. "Amongst our eternal hills," it reads, "we build a shrine, sans creed, sans dogma, inspiring all mankind." [5] Such shrines, however, neither inspire men nor heal their hurt nor correct their vision nor recenter their life. What Luther wrote of his fellow countrymen in the sixteenth century describes us now: "The common . . . people have no knowledge whatever of Christian teaching . . . and now that the Gospel has to be restored they have mastered the fine art of abusing liberty." [6]

If the demand for articulate doctrine as the base of a saving gospel is not powerfully apparent to Christian preachers, the opponents of Christianity know its pivotal character. Jean-Paul Sartre, convinced that God is dead, finds no possibility of taking his demise blithely, as if it did not matter. He writes:

[5] *Halford Luccock Treasury*, ed. Robert E. Luccock (Nashville: Abingdon Press, 1963), pp. 213-14.
[6] Small Catechism.

21

The existentialist finds it very troublesome that God does not exist, because with Him disappears all possibility of finding values in an intelligible world; . . . nor is it anywhere written that good exists, that we ought to be honest and not tell lies; for we are precisely on a plane where nothing exists but men.[7]

Bertrand Russell stands in similar case. It is possible, he reflects, to regard a difference about the taste for oysters as merely a matter of personal preference. When one is dealing with such grave matters as the Nazi torture of Jews, however, it is intolerable to have to say, "Cruelty is bad," and then be left with only some subjective preference for kindness as the ground for the judgment.[8]

Men can make such judgments only in terms of some firm reality on which they stand. For the Christian this is doctrinal teaching about the nature of the world as God's creation, of man as God's creature, of laws given by God's command, and of the dignity of all men as those "for whom Christ died." Short of the clear and forceful teaching and interpretation of this core of Christian truth, men are left to find their way in terms of such vague "spirituality" as left the self-styled "German Christians" of the Hitler era free to give allegiance to the Führer without acknowledging any break with Christ.

Freud protested against "philosophers who try to preserve the God of religion by substituting for him an impersonal, shadowy, abstract principle." In his indignation against such loss of grip on the articulate realities of the faith he rejected, he declared that for a little while he would like to be a be-

---

[7] Jean-Paul Sartre, *L'existentialisme est un humanisme*, p. 36, as quoted by John Baillie, *The Sense of the Presence of God* (New York: Charles Scribner's Sons, 1962), p. 38.

[8] *Ibid.*, p. 78.

liever, so that he could say to these faulty interpreters, "Thou shalt not take the name of the Lord thy God in vain." [9]

Doctrine clearly stated locates the living center of the gospel, and preaching that can save such a time as this must take seriously its obligation to teach the structural realities of the faith. One eminent theologian goes so far as to say that "exegesis and homiletics are as theological as systematics," since "theology is the methodical explanation of the contents of the Christian faith." [10] In every great age of preaching, ministers have taken this assignment in earnest. R. W. Dale, for instance, was both preacher and theologian, his stature as preacher resting to no small degree on his determination to make his theology live in his pulpit. His successor at Carr's Lane Church recalls that Dale not only published a strong theological treatise, *Christian Doctrine*, but gave all of it to his people from the Carr's Lane pulpit. The service of the congregation to civil and religious liberty, he added, was the outgrowth of their clear understanding of the teachings of the faith. Our off-center age urgently needs such a centered message.

Rival Doctrines Bid for Center

In the face of this challenge there is a third proposition: If Christian ministers do not center their preaching in doctrines clearly and powerfully taught, there can be no doubt that others will. A pulpit which trades in "the attractiveness of a studied amiability" leaves the way clear for the foes of Christ

[9] Will Herberg, in *Sermons to Intellectuals*, ed. Franklin H. Littell (New York: The Macmillan Company, 1963), p. 37.
[10] Paul Tillich, *Systematic Theology* (3 Vols.; Chicago: University of Chicago Press, 1951), I, 28.

to make converts. Men seek a ponderable structure of teaching concerning the meaning of life, and where we default in doctrine others move in to fill the vacuum.

Communism is a structure of doctrine. Though it issues in an economic theory and works through a political apparatus, its taproot is a system of doctrines making a basically religious interpretation of life's meaning. Based on a materialistic metaphysic, it holds a doctrine of man as an economic animal, to whom it proclaims a deterministic salvation, through the operation of an eschatology fabricated from the Hegelian dialectic of history, by the agency of the proletariat as chosen people, led by the messianic Party. It is not enough to meet such a system by political, economic, and military defenses. A former president of the Assembly of the United Nations said:

Naturally, if you are already converted to the materialistic standpoint of your opponents, you will argue with them only in terms of the gross national product, of raising the standard of living, of the rate of growth of the productivity of the nation, of social and economic justice, and of economic security and social benefits. The Communists love to confine you within that round of ideas.[11]

Within it you are confined, unless men are so instructed in the interpretation of life in the light of Christian doctrine that they are prepared to meet this system with the strong offensive of those who know emphatically what they believe.

Nazism was far more than political opportunism and military adventure. With its revival of Teutonic myth, its "leader principle," its conception of the Master Race, and its mysti-

[11] Charles Malik, *Christ and Crisis* (Grand Rapids: Wm. B. Eerdmans Publishing Co., 1962), p. 8.

cism of blood and soil, it was rooted in doctrine. Incipiently such a system is now in the making in the mysticism of the radical right and of the racist groups that proliferate in our age of tension. "Racism," as a recent message of the National Council of Churches pointed out, "must be understood for what it is—a religion competing with the Christian religion." It presents a doctrine of man involving "the condemnation of one race and the creative destiny of another by nature." [12] This is an ultimate claim as it relates to man and to the nature of the world in which he lives—in the real sense of the word, a religious claim which can flourish only when there is a vacuum of doctrinal preaching in Christian pulpits.

The fertility cult represented in much contemporary fiction and drama assumes doctrines that attempt to interpret life. The challenge in such a novel as *Lady Chatterley's Lover* is not in its frank portrayal of sex but in its implication that sex is itself the key to life's meaning. A couple who know almost nothing about each other as complete persons—whose minds meet only through a few snatches of fragmentary conversation —find such renewal of meaning in their existence through their sexual intimacies that they are willing to go away together in violation of the woman's marriage. At the book's end they are left proclaiming that in the proud expression of sex lies the redemption of our drab industrial society. Indeed, as their light-hearted quotation of one of the great psalms— giving it an unintended sexual meaning—implies, sex is the avenue to the divine. Since the book is not cheap pornography but the work of a writer of artistic stature, it is clear that such productions are a way of employing art for the presentation

[12] Race Relations Day message of the National Council of Churches, as reported in *The Christian Century*, Feb. 6, 1963, p. 166.

of doctrine which can be adequately met not by protest or censorship but by such Christian interpretation of life as can hold the field against its assailants.

In numerous guises and in the name of varied systems doctrine is preached. In a pulpit moratorium on doctrine, Christianity loses the battle by default; needless default, since its own doctrines clearly presented, thoughtfully interpreted, relevantly applied, have a creative and saving power no rival system can match. The ancient Deuteronomic Code contained an injunction apt to this hour: "You shall lend to many nations, but you shall not borrow" (Deut. 28:12). No borrower from the crusading paganisms which surround it, Christian faith is called rather to lend its strong understanding of life under God's governance and grace.

Mandate for Living Doctrine

All this issues in a final proposition: Preaching can meet the needs of this tumultuous day only as it recenters its message in vital Christian doctrine. Yet ministers have feared that doctrine might lack appeal and be dismissed as heavy and dry. Can this be true? In a congregation where on any Sunday the psychiatrist knows, if the preacher does not, many personalities are sick with guilt, can the doctrine of forgiveness be drab and unimportant? Among men and women returning from sickroom or graveside conscious of their mortality, is the doctrine of the Resurrection tiresome? When existentialism among intellectuals questions life's meaning, while many others are caught in a workaday whirl they call "the rat race," can the interpretation of life as held in the control of a wise and sovereign God be tiresome and irrelevant? Difficult the strong preaching of doctrine in the face of such challenges may be; dull and dry it is not.

Many a devout Christian feels a wistful hunger to know more of "what the church teaches." "When I talk about my religion with my Lutheran roommate," a student muses, "he seems to know much about his faith. Mine is important to me, but when I try to articulate it, it won't come into focus. I wish I knew more about the teachings of my church." An engaged girl laments, "When my fiancé and I talk about our plans as they relate to our religious life, he knows all about his Roman Catholic faith. My faith is precious to me—more so now than ever—but I can't explain it to him. I don't have the words. And while I *feel* it deeply, I don't really *know* enough about it myself." A successful lawyer, loyal to his church, says in deep seriousness, "I think our ministers ought to tell us more about theology. It's all very well to get an inspiring lift in church, but we laymen need to know far more than we do about the intellectual framework of our faith; and we're not likely to learn it unless our ministers help us."

These pleas sound no call to arid creedalism nor to the substitution of academic theological lectures for living, vibrant preaching. It is a misunderstanding of the function of doctrine to suppose that an emphasis on faith as it lives in a strong interpretation of the cardinal affirmations of the church is a commitment to dogmatism. The creed need not be an intellectual straitjacket; it can be a guide to the church's understanding of Scripture. It arose as the battle cry of the church as it faced the onslaught of paganism, and it can ring with rediscovered meaning in a day when paganisms of many kinds are again on the march.

Doctrine so preached meets urgent pastoral needs. Unless

27

he relates current life to basic doctrines, how can the minister help a man to answer the ever-present question, Who am I? Discovery of identity comes as a personal insight rising from one's own encounter with his Lord, but the path to that luminous moment is traced by the landmarks of doctrine by which he locates himself. When clear teaching, dramatized in a pulpit sensitive to current life, helps a man to see himself in relation to his Creator, his fall, his Savior and Elder Brother, his rebirth, and his eternal possibilities, he can no more live in tentative uncertainty about himself.

"On Being Who You Are" could be the title of such a pastoral sermon rooted in the puzzling life situation of many a modern gripped by the spiritual amnesia that has become epidemic in our civilization. It will lack effectiveness, however, unless it is also deeply doctrinal. It might be one way of preaching on the Incarnation from the text: "For God knew his own before ever they were, and also ordained that they should be shaped to the likeness of his Son, that he might be the eldest among a large family of brothers" (Rom. 8:29, NEB). The sermon could make two essential points:

1. This is who you are: Christ's full humanity reflects what you were made to be.

2. This is how you can become who you are: Christ's full divinity opens the way.

Such a sermon can etch the alternatives. Rejecting the possibilities opened in Christ, a man can live by the mechanistic interpretation of life common in our day. It lights the way dimly, however, as witness the brilliant Theodore Dreiser's summing up of his personal lostness: "As I see him, the unutterably infinitesimal individual weaves among the mysteries a floss-like and wholly meaningless course—if course it be. In short, I catch no meaning from all I have seen, and pass quite as I came, confused and dismayed." [13] Or like Thomas Wolfe, one can shortcut the momentous undertaking which Wolfe called "man's search to find a father, not merely the father of his flesh, not merely the lost father of his youth, but the image of a strength and wisdom external to his need and superior to his hunger, to which the belief and power of his own life could be united." [14] Wolfe attempted to satisfy this quest through human father-substitutes, in whom he trusted beyond their capabilities, of whom he demanded too much, and on whom he turned in the bitterness of his inevitable disappointment. Along such lines we cannot find ourselves. Let the sermon then explore the high meaning of life as we see it reflected in a real response to God as he comes to us incarnate in Jesus Christ. [15]

Not only pastoral but socially prophetic preaching finds strength in doctrine. Halford Luccock pointed to this source of power in his distinction between dealing with a sector of truth and an arc. "An arc," he reminded his students, "is a portion of the circumference of a circle; a sector is a V-shaped wedge in a circle, which includes a portion of the circumference but goes by radii to the center. 'Arc preaching" deals with a segment of the circumference of life; 'sector preaching' includes circumference but goes to the center." [16] The distinction is vital when the pulpit deals with social issues.

[13] As quoted by Walter Russell Bowie, *I Believe in Jesus Christ* (Nashville: Abingdon Press, 1959), p. 24.

[14] From *The Story of a Novel*, as quoted by Elizabeth Nowell in *Thomas Wolfe, a Biography* (Garden City: Doubleday & Company, Inc., 1960), p. 27.

[15] Chap. 6 further explores preaching on the Incarnation.

[16] Luccock, *op. cit.*, p. 147.

The minister holds no commission as sociologist or political analyst; he is called to speak of meanings that run to the core of existence, including social relationships but seeing them in terms of convictions about God, creation, redemption, the nature of man, and reconciliation effected on a Cross. Only such "sector preaching" can rise to the prophetic.

It wrought notable social change in the days of the Wesleys—change so shattering to the profits of men who lived by the exploitation of the weakness of their fellows as to make Wesley the most hated man, as well as the most loved, in England. In the face of workaday issues with starkly theological dimensions, preaching of this order is needed now. Witness the call for a theology of work in this age when automation is displacing men from the employment that gave meaning to their life; the need for a theology of leisure in a day when the unprecedented shortening of the workweek portends either creativity or deterioration; and the necessity for a theology of consumership in a time of economic abundance and the exploitation of men's responsiveness to the "hidden persuaders" evolved through motivation research.[17]

The real power of pulpit evangelism—to note but one further area—rests on a doctrinal substructure. Sin, grace, atonement, forgiveness, regeneration: these are the potent themes of the evangelist. It is a dark day for the church when the message is pitched on more opportunistic levels or when these themes are exploited without the depth imparted by a real probing of historic Christian teachings. Charles Haddon Spurgeon, memorable nineteenth-century evangelist, held that

[17] Cf. Ian G. Barbour, in *New Frontiers of Christianity*, ed. Ralph C. Raughley, Jr. (New York: Association Press, 1962), p. 39.

sermons have power to convert only when they deal meaningfully with such centered truths.

Not of evangelism only, but of all preaching designed to recenter our life, Spurgeon spoke the summarizing word. Pleading with preachers to move beyond surface discussions to the central truths of the faith, he urged: "Tell your hearers something, dear brethren, whenever you preach, tell them something, tell them something, tell them something." For preaching is not mere pleading, inspiration, refreshment from diverse sources. It is *telling*, and what it has to tell is centered in the core of what God has done for us in Christ, as the great doctrines of the church bring that home to us.

Such preaching, no mere recital of doctrine, is living confrontation, intimately related to men's affairs and dilemmas, rising from human experience and returning constantly to experience to throw light on the issues with which men grapple in their daily decisions. To the teaching task which makes doctrine thus commandingly alive, our quest for pulpit vitality now leads.

FOR FURTHER STUDY

Suggestions appended to these chapters seek to make this book more useful to students and working ministers. The reader who follows these indicated paths of investigation and practice will grow in his preaching by going beyond the accumulation of information to firsthand insights.

1. A few books, not full bibliographies but practical tools, suggested in each area offer starting points for further reading, guide lines for immediate pulpit work.

The reader's basic orientation will be aided by Theodore O. Wedel's *The Pulpit Rediscovers Theology* (Greenwich, Conn.:

The Seabury Press, Inc., 1956). Andrew W. Blackwood, *Doctrinal Preaching for Today* (Nashville: Abingdon Press, 1956) is rich in suggestion as to how preaching can serve this teaching task without losing evangelical urgency. My own *Preaching to the Contemporary Mind* (Nashville: Abingdon Press, 1963) stresses concern for specific aspects of contemporary lostness, coming back in each instance to a saving message rooted in some basic Christian doctrine. As an example of the doctrinal content of a "centered" gospel, James S. Stewart's *A Faith to Proclaim* (New York: Charles Scribner's Sons, 1953) is unsurpassed.

2. Homiletic skills grow only in preaching ventures. It is not too early to begin experimenting with outlines. The student might use the paragraphs on pp. 27-29 which deal with a doctrinal approach to pastoral preaching as a "starter" for a sermon "On Being Who You Are." No attempt has been made to develop the sermon within the bounds of this chapter, but a germinal idea is offered with a few suggestive materials. From this point of departure, why not detail an outline for a sermon you could preach in your own way?

3. Similar ventures in the treatment of evangelistic themes and social issues would be useful. Why not take a current social issue, clarify it as sharply as you can, define a Christian doctrine that speaks to it, work out a theme which expresses the dialogue between the need and the doctrine, and develop the idea into a sermon outline? Can you do the same with an aspect of human lostness and the evangelistic appeal of a central Christian teaching?

CHAPTER 2

Power
In a Teaching Pulpit

Make the Secret Plain

Too strenuously blazing trails for all who would one day interpret the gospel to have much thought for himself, Paul came at last to an hour of extremity when he wrote: "Include a prayer for us." A revealing need drove him to the request. "Include a prayer for us, that God may give us an opening for preaching." As if to make even more explicit the passion that drove him, he added: "Pray that I may make the secret plain." (Col. 4:2, 4 NEB) In prison, his one concern remained his teaching task, his prayer a teacher's yearning "that I may make the secret plain."

Had he not majored in this struggle our heritage would be sadly reduced—no churches, no lasting self-identity in a Christian message possessing sturdy continuity in its path

33

through the generations, no commanding Christology, no subjection of complex human relations to the single rule of Christ's lordship, none of the joyful springtimes of freedom for the spirit that have burst forth from age to age in fresh discoveries of the saving relation between law and grace. Paul's achievement as teacher passed God's gift in Christ through the channels of the mind to make it structural for the ages.

Every generation renews the call for gospel interpreters who winsomely teach. Charles E. Jefferson was haunted by a line from the story of the feeding of the multitude: "There is a lad here." "On entering your pulpit," he told his fellow ministers, "say to yourself, 'There is a lad here,' and for his sake, if not for your own, you must preach well." Momentous issues hang on it. For that lad, dull sermons mean dull religion. "You may have a church in which there is no millionaire," Jefferson reflected, "no professor, no author or painter or orator or scholar, no man or woman of cultivation or social prestige, but you will never be the pastor of a church in which there is not a boy, and that boy ought to be your salvation." [1] For more than thirty years at Broadway Tabernacle, Jefferson lived on the forward edge of Christian thought, deeply affecting the life of his time. One foundation stone of his influence was fidelity to his call to teach. Making things clear for the lad, he gripped men of stature and influence.

A transforming gospel must first lay hold on the mind. In *The Great Evangel*, Lynn Harold Hough's chapter titles march significantly: "The Evangel Which Masters the Conscience," "The Evangel Which Wins the Heart," "The Evangel Which

[1] *The Best of Charles E. Jefferson*, ed. Frederick Keller Stamm (New York: Thomas Y. Crowell Company, 1960), p. 180.

Speaks to the Whole Life." [2] The advance of such a gospel is toward a new day for men and society. But one first step precedes all these, "The Evangel Which Convinces the Mind." For the call to teach always lays a priority demand on the pulpit. The church's health, the continuity of the gospel, and the salvation of men and society hang on the faithfulness of preachers to that call.

Support the Lay Witness

One dimension of the ministry portrayed in the Pastoral Epistles reveals the concern of the early church with this matter. "If you put these instructions before the brethren," one such passage runs, "you will be a good minister of Christ Jesus, nourished on the words of faith and of the good doctrine which you have followed." (I Tim. 4:6.) "These instructions"! "Nourished on . . . good doctrine"! So from the beginning.

High priority in New Testament values falls to what is variously translated "doctrine" and "teaching." The words are next of kin, as the *Oxford English Dictionary* makes plain, defining doctrine as "the action of teaching or instructing; instruction; a piece of instruction; a lesson, or precept." Doctrinal formulations of the gospel which give it outline and make it teachable find early identity with the call to preach. So the epistle to Timothy continues: "Take heed to yourself and to your teaching [KJV: doctrine]; hold to that, for by so doing you will save both yourself and your hearers." (I Tim. 4:16.)

Generation by generation, this need recurs—always a new

[2] Dean Hough's Emory University lectures (Nashville: Cokesbury Press, 1935).

crop of babies who have not heard the gospel, new waves of young men and women who face a baffling world in which, if the message is to make sense, it must be taught in new grapplings with fresh knowledge and emerging issues. The faith must win the fight or perish. If it is true that our grand-fathers took Christianity in desperate earnest as the key to life's meaning, while our fathers took it more or less for granted and built their conduct on it without giving it much thought, and our generation passes it by as a dead issue, these premises do not tell us anything about the durable validity of the faith itself. They say, rather, that teachers have de-faulted in their responsibility to meet the minds of the on-coming generations. As old as the psalmist, with his in-junction,

> that you may tell the next generation
> that this is God,
> our God for ever and ever (Ps. 48:13-14),

this charge perennially abides.

Say as we will that lay witness, able to permeate the secular community, must renew the gospel's hold on our common life, the crucial responsibility for recruitment and training of this lay ministry falls necessarily to the minister of the Word. A practical division of labor assigns him leadership in think-ing through the meaning of the gospel in its dialogue with emerging issues, strange thought forms, and new areas of con-cern that erupt with new times. Only a strong teaching pulpit can make vital lay witness possible. The necessities of the church's life and the terms of his ordination make the minister a theologian to his parish.

It is not those who care little for Christian conduct who urge this priority for teaching. T. R. Glover could be accused of no carelessness about Christian behavior; yet note the vehemence with which he once said: "I don't give tuppence for the man who goes into the pulpit to tell me what my duty is: but I give all I have to the man who tells me from whence my help cometh." [3] Duty, Glover knew, is vitally important but never self-sustaining. It flourishes where its roots are nourished in doctrine.

Concerned Christians now ask searching questions about our life in society. "What can we do in the face of race prejudice and exclusions?" Wise men reply, "You can do much—after you learn who you are. To do something really helpful, you must be something. You will not long resist the pressures of a cruel secular society nor find your way among its confusions unless you have strong resources and a clear guide. Learn to say, 'I am a Christian,' not casually but as the most momentous fact of your existence. Learn to see what it means to be a Christian in these basic human relations. Fully clear on that, you can do much." Doctrinal clarity does not render practical steps self-evident; we still need wise social guides. But apart from self-understanding and commitment in the light of meaningful Christian faith, social skills are impotent.

Calling for saving changes in society, the World Council of Churches stressed this truth. Such impact, it said, "must come primarily from [the church's] influence upon its members through constant teaching and preaching of Christian truth in ways that illuminate the historical condition in which men

[3] William Russell Maltby, *Obiter Scripta*, ed. F. B. James (London: Epworth Press, 1952).

37

live and the problems which they face." [4] In meeting their social and civil responsibilities, the Amsterdam Assembly declared, men and women must learn to ask, "What does it mean to be a Christian in this situation?"

Apart from effective fulfillment of this teaching task, we are doomed to remain, as Elton Trueblood called us, a "cut-flower civilization," cherishing the bloom of Christian ethics gleaned along the way, which—severed from its root in Christian beliefs we have neglected to reinterpret and teach—withers and dies.

Teach with Continuity

Called to teach, the preacher lives under a mandate to plan his message with long continuity. Five reasons underscore this necessity.

First, the regular churchgoer has a right to a ministry which in the course of the year develops meaningful progression and cumulative power. No course of study in a good school could proceed on a merely day-to-day basis. Be the teaching philosophy ever so pupil-centered, articulate objectives must guide the work over a semester, setting individual lessons in a context which relates them to one another and to a meaningful encounter with a defined segment of truth. A series of isolated proclamations from texts chosen here and there according to the interests of the passing weeks inevitably misses this power. The churchgoer who has been in his pew forty Sundays during the year can look back on some helpful hours of inspiration but might be hard pressed to discern in the total experience a clearly defined Christian faith.

[4] Cf. report of the Amsterdam Assembly of the World Council of Churches.

Second, the gospel deserves a hearing in something approximating rounded wholeness. In its many-sided richness most ministers find some areas more commanding than the rest. Not by chance can the message come through with balanced fullness in the course of the year. Only by careful planning can the minister give adequate attention to subjects undeniably a part of the Christian heritage but not yet central in his outlook. Planned continuity alone can guard his congregation against his tendency to beat a monotonous path to the door of the gospel concerns dearest to his spontaneous zeal. Men sometimes look *back* over their preaching and attempt to correct its imbalance by changed emphasis; far truer is it to look *ahead* and lay out a plan of subjects for a year's time which can be tested in advance for unfortunate silences or the riding of hobbies.

Third, strong preaching can be sustained most dependably when the individual sermon comes as fruit of long growth rather than as product of quick assembly. When the minister has before him a plan of sermons for a longer period, a process of mental gestation sets in. Insight grows even when he is not actively at work on a given subject. Fragments from his reading, conversations with his people, observations by the way, thoughts while driving, meditations in the night —all throw light upon it. Subconscious forces enlist as allies. From time to time one subject or another comes to focus and begins to take shape. The preacher loses no time or nerve settling on what he is to speak about the coming Sunday; his preparation is guarded against hasty assemblies of undigested material; his creative powers are liberated for their fullest achievement.

Fourth, in a ministry growing in these silent, orderly ways, the preacher can render fullest stewardship of his powers. At least once a week he must stand before a congregation and reveal the contents of his mind. No man who respects either himself or his Lord dares to display a mind unfurnished. The necessities of the pulpit so magnetize his thinking and reading that his intellectual life and his preaching are indissolubly bound. If preaching is a week-to-week affair, his reading falls under pressure to follow its erratic thrusts. Then only a heavenly miracle can help him develop a mind organically whole; and God, whose creation sets a premium on orderly growth, does not seem disposed to deal in such miracles.

If, on the other hand, the preacher has projected a year's planned continuity, he need live no more under the tyranny of next Sunday. He can set up a simple file of the subjects on which he will preach in the next *fifty* Sundays, garnering material as he comes upon it. If faithful to his course in his study hours, he comes to each week armed with an arsenal of material gradually mobilized and with a mind prepared by long musing over the subject since first it was entered in the plan. Liberated from the anxious pressure of next Sunday's theme, he can read broadly and grow a stored and integrated mind.

Fifth, only by adequate planning can the preacher make the fullest use of the unparalleled opportunity for adult education which the pulpit puts within his reach. No other forum can match this advantage. A few radio and TV personalities reach a vast mass audience; but their hearing is spasmodic, subject to distractions, always "catch as catch can." Only for the Christian pulpit do a major portion of the people of every community in the land leave their homes once a week, gather at a place of assembly relatively free from distractions, and with time set aside for the purpose give respectful attention to something said to them about life's most important issues. To fritter away such an unrivaled opportunity on an unplanned and more or less random series of subjects, which make passing appeal to the preacher's interest or the public fancy, is nothing short of tragic. Yet such waste occurs in pulpits used only for "inspirational messages" or "refreshing the faith of the congregation." The preacher who takes seriously his ordination as a minister of the Word, planning carefully to meet his teaching responsibility, can most surely steward the opportunity God has given him.

Maintain the Dialogue

Not only does serious response to the call to teach summon the preacher to longtime planning; it plunges him into a thrilling dialogue between biblical doctrine and his people's need. On the one hand, it invites him to a fascinating adventure with his Bible and his notebooks. For the preparation of the year's plan does not begin with the calendar and a distracted search for enough subjects to fill fifty Sundays. It starts far back with an exploration of a fund of vital material out of which subjects can emerge.

One useful approach to the task makes it a treasured byproduct of the minister's devotional life. He takes one book of the Bible at a time—now a prophetic book, again an epistle, at some time during each year one of the Gospels—slowly making his way through it in daily segments. As he goes, he studies the material with such critical tools as he can master; devotional study has little value as mere sentimental brooding over the text. In his notebook he records the fruit of this study but does not stop with such analysis. As analyst he is

41

only observer, but he most needs that response in participation and decision in which saving revelation can occur. Of each day's reading he must ask, "What does this mean to me? Being who I am, where I am, with my temptations, sins, burdens, handicaps, opportunities, talents, what does this say to me? How am I involved? What response does it ask of me?" At this point he is not inquiring what he can preach from the passage but only how his Lord comes personally to him through its insights. Each day he records his discoveries in his notebook.

Day by day, his own life renewed, he goes forth to his ministry with strength replenished. The devotional discipline would be ample treasure if it offered nothing more, but a year later it yields its harvest of further dividends. Planning for the approaching year, the preacher rereads what is on deposit in his devotional notebook. Much he discards. Here and there a page unfolds possibilities that should be shared with his people, developed into a sermon to meet their needs as well as his own. These he marks for further study and possible incorporation into the year's plan.

All this is but one side of the dialogue. If planning calls the interpreter to his Bible, it calls also to a deepened attentiveness to his people's needs. Vital preaching grows out of double analysis of biblical text and contemporary life.[5] On

[5] I have dealt with double analysis in *Preaching to the Contemporary Mind* (Nashville: Abingdon Press, 1963). A key concept of that book, it is illuminated by many references but most fully developed in pp. 41-45, 96-99. "Valid preaching, as Professor John Knox points out, is not a circle drawn around a single center, either in exegesis of a biblical text or in address to contemporary need. It is rather an ellipse drawn around two foci: one in the text, the other in a current human situation" (p. 41). The process is illustrated by a double analysis of a biblical text and a current situation as portrayed in a contemporary novel, concluding: "So the possibilities of the

any given occasion, why does the minister preach from this text and not another? Among the themes and sermons that could be developed from the text, why does he preach this one? If something deeply vital happens in the preaching, the answer is probably that this sermon is part of a continuing dialogue between pastor and congregation. What is preached today brings to expression the message of the Word as, under the guidance of the Holy Spirit, a sensitive pastor has responded to the people's present need.

So the minister will have his people constantly before him as he lays out the plan for the year's preaching. He will think about individual parishioners and the peculiar circumstances that weigh upon them. He will think of groups in the church and what has been happening in their discussions and ventures in service—or their withdrawals from venturing. He will think about the total life of the parish and what its objectives need to be for the coming period. He will look out on the community and the nation and do his best to peer into the issues that bid fair to emerge in the next twelve months, keeping the focus on their demands and impingements upon his people. Strong preachers have always known that there are two sources of preaching insight—one in the library and the other in the parish—and that the preacher needs to learn about man from books and about individual men from intimate dealings in pastoral work. Preparing his plan, the preacher will keep all this warmly human insight in the forefront of his consciousness. Wherever he goes among texts, notebooks, ideas, reading, he will ask, "What does this say to my people's need?"

---

preaching message begin to emerge. The analysis of the text alone does not supply it. The analysis of contemporary life, in the parish or in the novel, does not provide it. But when the two analyses speak to each other, a theme and a message begin to come in view" (p. 45).

Working on the plan, he will live at the crossroads where these two streams of traffic meet: the one flowing from his Bible and his reading, the other from the life of the people. Watching the intersections of that traffic, he will struggle to formulate into challenging themes the clashes and tensions, the questions and answers, the offers and responses, the needs and fulfillments he finds occurring between God's Word and men's minds and affairs.

At last with the calendar before him, he will begin to fill in the Sundays of the coming year, noting the liturgical seasons and special days, and at last fitting the preaching themes he has been formulating into a progressive plan.[6] Somewhere during the year he may include an extended course of sermons in which he will spend two or three months preaching his way through a book of the Bible he has studied in the year just past. For some of the seasons he may turn to one of the lectionaries of the church for biblical material. In one or two shorter series of sermons he may make an approach to a synopsis of essential doctrines through the Apostles' Creed, the Lord's Prayer, the membership questions of his church, or sections of the Communion liturgy.

For the last part of the planning many ministers find it helpful to concentrate in a way they cannot do in the midst of parish demands and the preparation of the message for the coming Sunday. They save a portion of their vacation for this purpose or find some other way of having a few days apart for what amounts to a thrilling and creative spiritual retreat. They renew their joy and sense of urgency in the gospel

[6] See Chap. 4 for an interpretation of the Christian year in terms of the doctrinal emphases of the respective seasons and the light they throw on the devising of a preaching plan.

44

through the alluring vision of wholeness in the unfolding message which such a time affords.

A wise teacher once asserted that our colleges and universities are threatened far less by either radicals or conservatives than by "uninspiring teachers, . . . dispensers of branded canned goods." That is doubly true of the church and its ministry. The antidote, for college or church, lies in "untroubled periods of time when 'the wind bloweth where it listeth.' " [7] Such a time of attentive listening to the dialogue of the Word with the world enables the preacher to become a productive participant.

Focus the Creative Idea

Beyond longtime planning, the release of its potential requires of the pulpit a teaching approach to the preparation of each individual sermon. The preacher shares Paul's need: "Pray that I may make the secret plain." But when he has prayed, is there something more that he can do? Let an old maxim begin the answer: "Write yourself empty; read yourself full; think yourself clear; compose." That puts attention where it is needed most, not on the details of speech or sermon but on clarification of the germ idea.

One method by which to "write yourself empty" and "think yourself clear" is embodied in the steps of a useful worksheet. At each point the minister is closing in on the central idea from another significant direction. Not yet working out the details of the sermon, he is dredging up from his mental reserves significant matters that set forth the central idea. Each step is suggested by a single word.

[7] Zechariah Chafee, Jr., *The Blessings of Liberty*, as quoted by Gerald Kennedy, *A Second Reader's Notebook* (New York: Harper and Row, Publishers, 1959), p. 322.

First comes *"diagnosis."* Under this heading the preacher sets down the initials of at least a dozen persons with whom he has had pastoral dealings in the preceding week, setting opposite each some situation or need confronting that individual. Here a grief, there a temptation, a burden carried, a choice to be made, an opportunity hanging, an insensitivity in human relations, a frightening loneliness—the list grows before the minister until he sees sharply delineated a cross section of the congregation. Far different from generalizations about the plight of "man" or academic discussions of human need gleaned from books, this is the preacher's own fresh perception of *his people.* "To these listeners I must preach next Sunday," he reminds himself. "The sermon will do business with men and women like these, or it will do no business."

Working by plan, the preacher has conceived the idea of the sermon and collected much of its material long before. Over this bridge of "diagnosis" he now brings this treasure to the immediate situation. The portion of his preparation that falls within the week in which the sermon is to be preached begins with a fresh look at the mind and life of the people, because they cannot receive answers to questions they have not asked. Only when the message comes to them in terms that make them feel themselves participants, will it have the luminous quality of revelation.[8]

His "diagnosis" completed, the preacher sets down the second heading of his worksheet, *"prescription."* Reviewing the personal needs he has just listed, he tries to visualize something of what the gospel might bring to each. He cannot pretend to have answers for all their problems, and he knows

[8] Tillich, *op. cit.,* II, 13.

that if saving insight comes it must rise out of their own encounter with truth. Yet he cannot escape the responsibility, as their shepherd, to search for some realistic glimpse of what the gospel brings to their need. For each he writes a brief statement of some step in healing or growth that might emerge if this circle of friends could share a quiet talk together.

Moving to his third heading, "exposition," the preacher looks once more at the scripture on which he has planned to preach. Though he studied the text when he first planned this sermon as part of the year's pilgrimage, he goes back to it now, probes it again, examines it in the light of the needs he has just been facing, inquires what fresh word it has to say to these needs, and finally checks all that he has done against the best commentaries to which he has access, distilling his discoveries in his worksheet.

Whereupon he is ready for his fourth heading, "experience." In a weekly confessional in the light of the truth he is preparing to preach, the minister examines himself. "What does this mean personally to me?" he asks. "Do I deeply believe it? Have I been living by it? If so, what has it done through me? Am I sinning against it? Where I fall short of its standard, what has been the cost to others and to me?" The findings of such self-searching may not often appear in a sermon, but the minister will preach with deeper understanding and greater urgency for having examined himself in this way. If such personal scrutiny seems to any man needless bother, it may interest him to note that other workers, bound only by artistic necessity, regard it of first importance. John van Druten declares as a basic rule for a successful playwright: "Write only of what you really know. Never write unless you

47

feel." [9] This review of his own experience with the truth he proclaims is the preacher's way of making sure he is talking about what he really *knows* and that he *feels* afresh through vivid recall.

A fifth heading reads, "*program.*" Here the preacher is at pains to clarify in his own mind some specific, desired outcomes of this truth in the lives of his people. A young woman once explained her absence from her own church by saying she had been going to hear a neighboring pastor, "because," she said, "he has such workable sermons." Not all preaching can be reduced to a few simple "how-to-do-it" steps, yet men and women are hungry to know in reasonably specific terms where they may *begin* to make use of what comes to them in the gospel. The wise preacher knows how to put at least a few "handles" on the truth he teaches. Under the word, "program," the minister sets down some things he could say to a man who might respond: "Pastor, that message got me. What do I do now?"

Sixth on his worksheet the minister writes, "*purpose.*" Here he must determine his course among the rhetorical possibilities. While all sermons are aimed to help precipitate the saving encounter with God, not all reach the goal over the same route. Some come to it through *instruction*; some are aimed to *convince*; others are designed to *motivate, persuade, inspire*; still others appeal for *specific action*. Among these purposes the minister marks his way in a brief statement.

To complete the worksheet he writes his seventh heading, "*proposition.*" The foregoing steps have prepared him to put the whole sermon idea in one clear sentence such as com-

---

[9] James McBride, a review of *Playwright at Work*, by John van Druten, the New York *Times*.

petent workmen in other fields require of themselves. John van Druten put it simply in another of the rules that enabled him to turn out strong plays at the rate of nearly one a year: "Keep your theme fluid until the last possible moment, but frame it in a single declarative sentence before you put a word on paper." [10] One way to grasp the importance of this matter is to see what happens when an artist fails to take it seriously. Thomas Wolfe's literary genius made it possible for him to produce memorable books, but only with much fumbling and personal agony for all who were associated with him. In writing *Of Time and the River* he took four years, wrote approximately a million words, though only a fraction of that number could be used in the book, and finally finished only because his editor almost literally took the manuscript away from him and supervised the cutting and rearranging of the material. His biographer notes that after a year of work on the novel and the writing of many thousands of words, Wolfe still had not decided what its main theme was to be.[11]

Creative genius and the patience of his editor, Max Perkins, enabled Wolfe to produce in spite of a bad method. Not granted four years between productions, the preacher needs a method which dependably brings the sermon into form. The key is a well-constructed proposition; in van Druten's words, "Frame it in a single declarative sentence before you put a word on paper." This sentence announces the one central affirmation from which all else stems and which every paragraph will in some way clarify, explain, develop, or support.

A news item dramatized these urgencies. It told of a thirteen-year-old Kansas City girl who shot both her parents. All

[10] *Ibid.*
[11] As related by Nowell, *op. cit.*

49

she wanted to do, she told reporters, was to break up a fight between them. "I just shot," she explained. "I didn't aim at anyone. I just tried to keep Daddy from hitting Mother." Feeling the poignant sorrow of that family crisis, one cannot escape the truth that though the girl's motive was laudable her aim was poor. It is folly to pull the trigger before you know what you aim to hit.

The parable raises questions for every preacher. Is my desire to serve the Lord enough if I have not clarified my aim? What am I aiming at—and whom? Are the disciplines I follow adequate to give me the sharp aim needed in clear Christian teaching? A memorable preacher of the last century declared, "It is not enough to be so plain that you can be understood; you must speak *so that you cannot be misunderstood.*" [12] Such clarity employs words as faithful and accurate servants of meaning. Chap. 3 will explore how words and meanings are linked in living experience to bring saving doctrine to a vital pulpit.

FOR FURTHER STUDY

1. *Design for Preaching,* by H. Grady Davis (Philadelphia: Fortress Press, 1958), makes an original contribution in clarifying the sermon idea. *In the Minister's Workshop,* by Halford E. Luccock (Apex ed.; Nashville: Abingdon Press, 1944), gives many-sided guidance in a sparkling style calculated to kindle creative imagination.

2. Much can be learned by analysis of doctrinal sermons. For varied methods of doctrinal preaching, see James S. Stewart's *The Strong Name* (New York: Charles Scribner's Sons, 1941); George

[12] Charles H. Spurgeon, *Encounter with Spurgeon,* ed. Helmut Thielicke (Philadelphia: Fortress Press, 1963), p. 91. Italics added.

A. Buttrick's *So We Believe, So We Pray* (Apex ed.; Nashville: Abingdon Press, 1951); and my own *Creed of Our Hope* (Nashville: Abingdon Press, 1954).

It will be helpful to make a careful study of the method employed by each of these preachers, as it is revealed by working through several sermons:

(a) Make an outline of the sermon showing the introduction and conclusion in detail and the main points with at least the major subpoints.

(b) If you can find the proposition (see pp. 48 ff. stated in the preacher's own words, set it down. If he has not given a concise statement of it, work out a single declarative sentence in which you state the main thrust of the sermon.

(c) Which of the rhetorical purposes (see p. 48) do you consider paramount here?

(d) Can you find indications of the human needs the preacher attempted to meet? Set down such traces of the "diagnosis" (see pp. 46 ff.) as you discern in the sermon.

(e) How does the preacher relate this doctrine to the Scripture? Is it textual? topical? expository? Do you find his exegesis adequate? Would a different biblical orientation be more helpful?

(f) Write a brief critique of the sermon as to its general impression, its truth, its sense of urgency.

3. The sermon projects suggested in these chapters will profit by use of the worksheet process (pp. 45-49). Why not begin by putting it to work as you prepare your next sermon?

4. Now would be a good time to begin the advance preparation for a program of planned preaching scheduled to commence a year from now. Why not take some book of the Bible and begin the kind of notebook study proposed on pp. 41 ff.? This will take time each day and will have value in proportion to the disciplined regularity with which it is sustained. Its rewards, both in spiritual enrichment and in help to next year's preaching, can be immense.

CHAPTER 3

Words
In Search of a Meaning

Linking Meaning to Experience

In a provocative play, Luigi Pirandello portrays "Six Characters in Search of an Author." The scene is laid in an empty theater where a stock company prepares to rehearse a routine production. Into this commonplace setting burst six people from the real world outside, demanding a hearing. A tangled skein of events, in which weakness and nobility intermingle, has brought their family relations to a sorry plight, plunging some dagger of shame or bitterness into the heart of each. The story has happened to them, and they seek help to put it on the stage to enlighten an audience.

When the company's manager consents to undertake the production, complications arise. Since a play is more than the simple reenactment of raw events before the footlights, he puts his professional actors into the respective roles to heighten and intensify the real life drama. But the original "characters" display deep distress, feeling themselves not fully understood nor truly represented. One of them demands who these actors are, to take such liberties with his personal experience as he knows it from within. As a *character*, he insists, he has a right to ask the *man* who portrays him, who he *is*. For a character has his own life, "marked with his especial characteristics." [1]

Though our present context forbids further pursuit of the action, with its profound reflections on the bond of life with art, this much of the plot presents a symbol of the relation of speech to experience. Words are not meanings in any constant sense, like coins which pass from hand to hand with unaltered value. Possessing no independent existence, they point to what lies beyond them. Experience provides the "story" of which words as "actors" seek to bring the meaning to the stage. It need astonish no one that they fall short of adequate portrayal of the real-life drama. To paraphrase Pirandello, an experience has a right to ask a word "who" it is, because an experience has its own life, marked by its distinctive meaning.

This link is crucial to the preacher. With words as tools he must open doors to experience in areas of highest importance, where issues of life and death are joined. Though, in Goethe's phrase, "the highest cannot be spoken," he is called to convey the highest and to do so by speaking. Words in search of a meaning, meanings in search of a word, this

---

[1] Luigi Pirandello, "Six Characters in Search of an Author," *Naked Masks*, ed. Eric Bentley (Everyman's Edition; New York: E. P. Dutton & Co., Inc., 1922, 1950), Act III, p. 265.

troubled commerce of words with meanings comprises his daily field of labor.

Abstractions tempt him to violate the pact between words and experiences. Nurtured long in schools, a companion of books, he is lured away from the action-filled speech of living men. One hears a preacher talking jargon about something that extends "from the creation to the eschaton"—what is the man in the pew to make of that? Pulpit language makes free with salvation, justification, sanctification, incarnation, resurrection, grace—abstractions all! *Unless drawn from experience, the words themselves manifest no action to the listener.* Even "man"—favorite generalization of preachers and theologians—is not plain, everyday John Smith. Under the anonymity of this blanket term, John Smith's Sunday-morning complacency remains undisturbed even by the dire announcement that "man" is a lost sinner.

To decry abstractions is not to plead that pulpit vocabulary be stripped bare of these words. The preacher, knowing their true worth, must learn to dole them out with miserly reluctance to lay them on the counter of free-spending speech. Words, like coins, depreciate in value with inflationary spending. Christianity's key words need a restoration of value; men cannot make sense of their Bibles unless such terms as "justified," "saved," "resurrected," "grace," and a host of others recover rich meaning which links them with vital experience.

So essential is this link that a minister's inability to express his theology without the language of the classroom marks him not as profound but as less than master of his theology. Technical terms echo by rote what he has heard or read, but theology is not books; it is life. Technical language is professional shorthand among the initiated; truth is not imprisoned in its words. New Testament truth is what men *do* in the life from which the words are abstracted, and we do not know our theology if the words hold us captive, helpless to find our way back to the living experience and say the thing in our own way in the salty speech of common men.

A persuasive contemporary preacher has branded academic speech as the dead language of men who talk like walking ghosts. Only "in the marketplace, the home, at the ball park, the shop, the church," he says, is language alive.[2] For in these places men come close to *things, actions, persons*. Only those who drink at these springs will refresh their language with the cool reality of concrete events.

Delegates to a Christian youth conference in Berlin in 1960 were given opportunity to discover firsthand the hard toil of speaking truth simply. Studying the epistle to the Ephesians, they were asked to put its message into a newspaper letter on the subject of peace. One youth concluded it would be easier to write a book on systematic theology! Of course it would. For systematic theology, as D. T. Niles observed, is rubric for the temple, not required to make itself clear to the uninitiated, whereas a newspaper letter demands conversation with wayfarers on the road.[3]

Preaching calls for conversation that points to crucial experience. Language not freshly drawn from life situations fails in this assignment, and may even be a work of the devil—as David Head's "Satan in Disguise" implies in his prayer: "May they communicate their message with the utmost zeal, in

[2] Gerald Kennedy, *While I'm on My Feet* (Nashville: Abingdon Press, 1963), p. 24.
[3] *Upon the Earth* (New York: McGraw-Hill Book Co., Inc., 1962), p. 74.

words no one else can understand." [4] This may be another instance of sons of this world being wiser than the sons of light (Luke 16:8)! For it gives Satan's inverted twist to a truth that every preacher must learn with the intensity of second nature, to wit: In a vital pulpit, doctrinal preaching maintains an unbroken link with living experience from which doctrine arises and to which it returns with needed ethical guidance.

From Experience to Doctrine

Persuasive preaching of a doctrine brings into view the experience from which it arose, for valid doctrine is a way of reporting experience and guiding others to share it. When it oversteps this function, it invites distrust. Cyprian, for instance, teaching that saving grace comes through the sacraments, was building solidly on his experience in baptism. When he took the further step of ruling that saving grace can come *only* through the sacraments, he went beyond experience into uncharted areas of speculation.[5]

Against the wild hazards of such ventures, W. G. Sumner protested that they make trouble by cutting human relations adrift as derelicts on stormy seas of quarreling over words. "If you want a war, nourish a doctrine," he warned. "Doctrines get inside of a man's own reason and betray him against himself. Civilized men have done their fiercest fighting for

---

[4] *Shout for Joy* (New York: The Macmillan Company, 1962), p. 48.

[5] Cf. Arthur John Gossip in *The Interpreter's Bible*, VIII, 569 ff. In this connection H. Richard Niebuhr [*Christ and Culture* (New York: Harper & Row, Publishers, 1951), p. 238] has recourse to a similar principle: Men are usually right in what they affirm, less dependable in what they deny. For, unlike their denials, their affirmations rise from direct experience.

doctrines." [6] One has only to recall the disastrous conflict between Christian and Moslem civilizations or Europe bled white in the warfare of Catholics with Protestants or the hazardous Cold War between East and West to feel the cogency of his protest. Verbalized doctrines are costly luxuries unless men keep discussion linked to sources in experience.

This insight underlies the semanticist's insistence that all use of language must penetrate abstractions to an "operational referent"—something overt, something done, of which one man can say to another: "Here, this is what I mean. Come and check it for yourself." [7] In terms of familiar New Testament material, this means pushing past the generalization, "publicans and sinners," to look long and squarely at a man like Zacchaeus; or seeing through the phrase, "scribes and Pharisees," to such a man as Nicodemus. When we turn from the label—always an abstraction—to the man who enters into vivid experience, doors of mutual understanding begin to open. So Jesus constantly pushed past labels to persons.

Until this happens we fall into the trap of mistaking inference for description. Stuart Chase cites the faulty syllogism:

> Stags run fast.
> Some Indians run fast.
> Some Indians are stags.[8]

---

[6] War, as quoted in A New Dictionary of Quotations, compiled by H. L. Mencken (New York: Alfred A. Knopf, Inc., 1942), p. 299.

[7] Stuart Chase makes use of this principle at many points in The Tyranny of Words (Harvest ed.; New York: Harcourt, Brace & World, Inc., 1938).

[8] Ibid., p. 88.

The first two lines supply descriptions and are true; the last, an inference from them, is false. The matter ceases to be harmlessly academic when it is rephrased in terms not unfamiliar today, even in high places of political influence.

> Communists advocate equal rights for all races.
> Martin Luther King advocates equal rights for all races.
> Martin Luther King is a Communist.

Here again two true descriptions blur into one false conclusion. Men schooled in logic know some principles for detecting such fallacies, but there is constant need to get back of labels, that grow out of such abstraction from life, to the operational referent in direct observation.

"Find the referent"—a maxim which, according to Chase, states "the goal of semantics"—provides the preacher with a needed rule.[9] The wise gospel interpreter constantly refers his message to firsthand occurrences sufficiently concrete to enable him to say, "This is what I mean. Come and check it for yourself." This need not bind him in the straitjacket fashioned by the logical empiricists with their dictum that "every factual proposition must refer to *sense-experience*" or otherwise be branded as merely "emotive" use of language.[10] On such grounds the Russian cosmonaut dismissed faith as absurd because he caught no glimpse of God in outer space.

When the preacher speaks of experience, he insists that he need not be confined to the physical senses and that the word "sense" has a broader meaning than this usage implies. He

[9] *Ibid.*, p. 9.
[10] Alfred Jules Ayer, *Language, Truth, and Logic* (New York: Dover Publications, Inc., 1946), p. 71. Italics added.

takes seriously John Baillie's reminder of such other valid terms as "common sense," "sense of humor," "sense of beauty," "sense of honor," "sense of duty," "sense of the divine." Though not quite as tangible as sight and touch, these provide avenues to bona fide experiences which enable us to know something we should otherwise miss.[11]

As validly as other disciplines appeal to the senses, gospel interpretation turns to its own distinctive kind of experience. Baillie cites the analogy of the judgment that a piece of music is beautiful. It can be checked only by returning to the experience from which it orginally rose. One must hear the music again and again, live with it, bring to bear on it such music theory as he can master, compare his appreciation of it with that of others, including the musical experts, until out of the total experience some consensus emerges. Validity is confirmed in such a judgment by experience which includes the senses but goes far beyond them to yield its own kind of knowledge.[12]

Doctrinal judgments, by the same token, have a right to claim validity when they stand the test of repeated checking by return to the kind of experience from which they emerged. They cannot be denied access to such "referents" simply because the experiences involved are not fully describable in sense terms. Arthur Eddington was right in his parable of the zoologist who gathered ocean specimens with a net made on a two-inch mesh and concluded there are no fish in the sea smaller than two inches! Insisting on the *right* of access to religious experience as valid data from which to draw his doctrine, the minister must accept the *necessity* of keeping the

[11] *Op. cit.*, pp. 55 ff.
[12] *Ibid.*, pp. 63 ff.

link with experience so solidly forged that he can look with his hearers at vital occurrences drawn from the Bible, from biography, and from current affairs, of which he says: "Here, this is what I mean. Come and check it for yourselves."

From Scripture to Living Men

Preaching glows with vitality when the Bible is seen not as a compendium of abstract ideas but as an avenue of encounter with living experience. Scriptural doctrine speaks less frequently in generalized statements than in parables, prayers, historic events.

The luminous experience known to great religion as revelation seldom appears in a formula, caught in a net of words, packaged, and delivered. It inheres in memorable episodes through which a man sees what his life, or some part of it, means. In Ian T. Ramsey's phrase, there is a "disclosure, the penny drops, the light dawns." [13] Whereas scientific language is constructed on mathematical "models," religious language rests on "models" of concrete personal relationships.[14] These supply the material of preaching, finding classic and normative expression in the Bible, coming within the reach of men's own firsthand affairs.

Real experience resists our whims. It refuses to shape itself to our wishes. "Reality," as John Baillie remarked, "is 'what I come up against!' " [15] Is not this a notable feature of our life with the Scriptures? They will not bend to our desires.

[13] These terms comprise a recurring refrain in Professor Ramsey's *Religious Language* (Macmillan Paperbacks Edition; New York: The Macmillan Company, 1963).

[14] Cf. Albert N. Wells, *The Christian Message in a Scientific Age* (Richmond: John Knox Press, 1962), pp. 56 ff.

[15] *Op. cit.*, p. 33.

They call us back from mystic raptures to the hard challenge of ethical issues. They confront our matter-of-fact rationality with miracle and mystery. Against our earthy assumption that men must earn their salvation they hurl the assertion that only grace through faith can save us. On every page stubbornly resistant reality presents itself and in the *presenting* shows itself not past or future but *present*. The Bible comes alive when in double analysis with the experience of living men it is seen as no mere record of things done long ago and far away, but a pointer to unrealized dimensions of the living present.

Thus the text stands forth as "paradigmatic experience." [16] The truth it reports, not confined to a story of happenings "once upon a time," makes contact with what is true always and everywhere. Through the text as interpretive symbol the hearer can grasp meaning and potential in his own experience, and the invitation to make that adventure is the purpose of the scripture and the point of the sermon.

James S. Stewart's sermon on "The Strong Name of the Trinity" provides a case in point. From his text, "The grace of the Lord Jesus Christ, and the love of God, and the communion of the Holy Ghost, be with you all" (II Cor. 13:14 KJV), Stewart moves with dispatch to the crucial declaration "that in its origins the doctrine of the Trinity came . . . straight out of the experience of ordinary men and women." As if fearful lest this statement be lost, he recasts it and says it again in the next sentence: "It did not spring from the dexterous manipulation of abstract ideas: it sprang from the presence of concrete facts and realities."

A moment later he asks, "Why should not we, in this mat-

[16] *Ibid.,* p. 75.

ter, be as simple and direct as the New Testament, as factual and experimental as the Christians of the early Church?" So, treating what often appears to be one of the most abstruse of Christian doctrines, Stewart—strong theologian that he is —holds it close to concrete experience. From beginning to end, this vital sermon presses the matter back to the truth that the Trinity is the name which Christians have found best designed to recall the ways in which they have met God. In theme sentences which, with slight rephrasing, he repeats again and again, Stewart says: "I beg you . . . to get right back to what is simple and direct and your very own. Is it not true that you cannot say all that is contained for you in the word 'God,' until you have said Father, Son, Spirit? This is to believe in the Trinity." [17] From this base in experience he launches the three main sections of the sermon through the respective phrases of the text, reconstructing the dealings with God which they represented in the early Church and to which they can lead now.

Turning from study of this classic example, let the preacher venture his own double analysis of text and experience to preach on the central Protestant doctrine of justification by faith. He may well begin with a word study on the verb "to justify" and its Greek forebear, *dikaioo*. Dictionaries and Bible commentaries startle his awareness that "to justify" is not "to make just" but "to restore a broken relation"—with all that this means concerning transformation of ethical conduct when the relation to a righteous God is renewed. But he will go beyond this to a double analysis which takes him into the experience of present-day men and women.

[17] *The Strong Name* (New York: Charles Scribner's Sons, 1941), pp. 251-54.

Pastoral care of his people may have led him to some parishioner bound in a chain of obsessive guilt. Pastoral calls may have been marked by a long sequence of confessions probing farther and farther back into the yesterdays, seeking forgiveness for every individual misdeed. Assured of pardon again and again, this lost soul has never felt forgiven. In this context it grows clear that forgiveness is not commerce about so many separate *deeds* but acceptance of a *person*. Thus in justification God restores the broken relation.

These reflections lead to recollection of a hospital patient whose recovery from surgery crept through agonizing delay conditioned not by physical complications but by depletion of inner energies, a depression which seemed related to troubled brooding over having failed a brother now dead and beyond reach for his forgiveness. There is need for something more total and far-reaching than the piecemeal forgiveness dependent on human frailty and mortality. This justification gives; beyond all partial restorations there is One, who represents life in its totality, who accepts us. Restored to a true relation with him, we can come to a sense of rightness with life itself, a healing wholeness.

The minister remembers a conversation in which a parishioner said to him: "These were my reasons for acting as I did. Don't you think I was justified?" This friend's insistent need that another approve his attempt to put himself in the right displayed how impossible such self-justification proves to be. Not even with another failing mortal can we reestablish a broken peace by such proofs of our rightness. Only when the other accepts us—not our arguments—can the right relation be restored. How much less can we put ourselves in the right with God on any basis short of his acceptance.

63

Examining the estrangements of his people from one another, from what they know as their true selves, and from
God, the minister sees that these lost ones need the healing
that comes by faith, not as intellectual belief only but as a
total response to God's acceptance of them as it is symbolized
in Christ's self-sacrifice on the cross. Double analysis turns
now to a text: "Since all have sinned [and are thus estranged,
separated] and fall short of the glory of God, they are justified
[restored from brokenness to a total wholeness in all their relations—with themselves, with others, and with God] by his
grace as a gift [not a *quid pro quo*, so much forgiveness for so
much confession], through the redemption [the release of a
whole person, not the kind of arrangement that deals with
isolated acts one by one] which is in Christ Jesus." (Rom.
3: 23-24.)

Double analysis makes vivid a truth which could not come
home to the preacher with the same gripping quality of immediacy when read in academic abstractions—the truth that
the broken relationships which haunt and burden us can be
restored by accepting the fully right relation God has already
offered in the acceptance evidenced in Christ. From such experiences the biblical doctrine rose; in return to them it can be
persuasively preached.

Product and Guide of Experience

In a vital pulpit, doctrine thus freshly grasped as rooted in
experience returns to experience with ethical guidance. Paul's
letters supply the model. For they achieve ethical strength
not by whipping the wills of men but by lighting up conduct
with great doctrine clearly taught. Writing to Philemon
about his Christian duty toward a runaway slave or to the

church at Corinth concerning the gross immoralities of some of its members, Paul speaks first of their relation to God in Christ. From this base he advances to implications concerning behavior becoming to those who are "in Christ."

The epistle to the Romans—ripest statement of New Testament doctrine, fountainhead of the great theologies of Christendom—makes this evident. The letter glows with a winsome statement of Christian ethics beginning at the twelfth chapter, entered over the bridge of the word "therefore." "I appeal to you therefore, brethren, by the mercies of God, to present your bodies as a living sacrifice, holy and acceptable to God, which is your spiritual worship." (12:1.) Paul has worked his way through the unfolding structure of Christian doctrine culminating in the doxology which concludes the eleventh chapter. Then, without pausing to catch his breath, he bursts out with "therefore" and is off in his discussion of how Christians conduct themselves. For him the gospel imperative concerning conduct rises naturally and directly out of the gospel indicatives concerning doctrine. The two organic parts form a living whole.

Emil Brunner holds that this ethic is the goal of the whole letter. No afterthought tacked on in a postscript, it is the flowering of all that Paul's vision of the faith implies. God lays claim not to men's thinking only; he will settle for nothing short of will and act. But will and act, powerless to sustain themselves, require guidance and motivation drawn from the luminous insights conveyed by doctrine. The ethics grow out of the dogmatics, as the fruit comes from the sap of the tree.[18]

[18] Emil Brunner, *The Letter to the Romans* (Philadelphia: The Westminster Press, 1959), p. 101.

Living issues in this complex age demand this power. It supplies the primary strength in R. Frederick West's helpful book, *Preaching on Race*. Dr. West handles this explosive issue in the light of the realization that "we must deal with overwhelmed people, not buckets of overwhelming facts." Never short on facts, he knows that in preaching he deals primarily with the spiritual needs of the people who hear the message. "At rock bottom," he asserts, "the race problem is not merely the apparent different colors of human skin, but the variety of subtle layers of human sin." Sermons which the author preached in the social milieu of the Deep South speak forthrightly to the social issue, yet repeatedly they find their strength in the doctrinal positions which underlie their message. "The genuine sermon involving race will involve all persons in a more ultimate Christian concern about their own attitudes and actions by fresh encounters with God." [19]

What the race issue demonstrates in one troubled area, most ethical decisions underscore. A well-worn maxim enjoins that "doctrines are to be preached practically, and duties doctrinally." Where this connection holds firmly, men find the way out of the ethical relativities that threaten to engulf us. Speaking of people who have no solid ground for discerning where their duty leads, William E. Sangster put the matter memorably. For them, he said:

Morality is convention. If under duress they connect it with God at all, they do so with hesitation and confusion. If they have tried to think the matter through, they have concluded that "morals" are customs which people in time past have found socially convenient but which have no real and ultimate sanction.

[19] (St. Louis: The Bethany Press, 1962), pp. 26-31.

At a pinch they can be jettisoned. Tired of the same face over the breakfast table, you can go off with someone else. If what has proved socially convenient in time past proves now to be personally inconvenient, well—you need not be held by it. Nothing has eternal meaning. "What's right or wrong but thinking makes it so?" So think the way you like! Let changing desire be your erratic guide and recognize in your rare moments of lucidity that you are like a mariner lost on an uncharted ocean without a compass or a rudder.[20]

Exhortations about what they *ought* to do cannot help such people. Their problem lies in loss of belief that *ought* itself has any meaning. What reason, then, can prompt change in behavior? Only strong teaching about ultimate reality can break the circle of their self-enclosed moral relativity. To preaching is assigned the crucial task of preparing a mind in which men see their lives as inseparably related to God who made them, to Christ who redeemed them, to the Holy Spirit who can give them a new life unfolding in power beyond their own, and to an eternity of which the fleeting span of their earthly years comprises one small segment.

Yet such doctrinal preaching calls for plain speaking on current issues in language all men understand. It is possible to say the true word so abstrusely that it makes no effective impact. Helmut Thielicke suggests how a Christian in Hitler's Third Reich might have spoken with comparative safety. As some Nazi minion launched his anti-Christian tirade in the Berlin Sportspalast, a believer might have shouted from his place in the stands: "Christ is the Messiah." Beyond a few scornful glances from the people seated near him, there

---

[20] *Power in Preaching* (Nashville: Abingdon Press, 1958), p. 80.

would have been no effect. But suppose he were to have risen in his place and called out a theological equivalent phrased in words that bite into contemporary experience: "Jesus Christ is the only Lord, and all who make themselves into gods by their own power will go to hell along with the pseudo-savior Adolf Hitler." [21] This witness might have cost his life but its meaning would not be lost. Such translation of doctrine into the language of experience supplies the essentials of ethical guidance and the power of a vital teaching pulpit.

Gerald Kennedy, reflecting the pulpit's urgent need for the sharply precise use of words, protests against devotional writing that capitalizes such words as "Light," "Spirit," "Truth," with a seeming assumption that the capital letter eliminates the need for clear definition. Even where exact definition is not possible, he remarks, tossing the words out unrelated to concrete reference points in experience "is like trying to sell moonbeams in Woolworth's." [22] A vital pulpit shuns such anomalies by maintaining an unbroken link with experience from which doctrine arises and to which it returns with needed ethical guidance.

From this need to link word to meaning through experience, a significant question emerges: To what central "referent" can Christian experience make dependable appeal? Obviously not to a chaotic mass of individual subjectivity to which no standard has been applied. Where, then, shall the preaching turn to find not "moonbeams at Woolworth's" but an authentic yardstick by which to approach both biblical and personal experience?

The New Testament "kerygma" best supplies this need.

[21] Spurgeon, op. cit., p. 34.
[22] While I'm on My Feet, p. 22.

In the remaining chapters we must give sustained attention to this preaching of the apostles and its relation to the full expression of the gospel. If one approaches the kerygma with merely antiquarian interest in the life of the first-century church or with merely orthodox bent to measure theological correctness, its contribution will be meager. But suppose these insights concerning the kerygma were to become as many highroads leading straight into the experience of the apostles with their Lord—what could be more exciting or important? The apostolic witness, thus freshly encountered, leads to experience of a living Christ. For this high adventure Chap. 4 charts a beginning.

FOR FURTHER STUDY

1. Study of semantics will reward the preacher. Stuart Chase, *The Tyranny of Words* (Harvest ed.; New York: Harcourt, Brace & World, Inc., 1938), provides a practical introduction, no less stimulating because it challenges the preacher's philosophical positions. John Baillie's Gifford lectures, *The Sense of the Presence of God* (New York: Charles Scribner's Sons, 1962), offer a thoughtful answer to the positivism which runs through much semantic literature, as well as a bracing venture in reflective thinking concerning the relation of Christian doctrine to experience.

2. This would be a good time to begin the exploration of some body of Christian affirmation for its doctrinal preaching values. Such materials as the Apostles' Creed, the service for receiving members into your church, or the service of baptism or Holy Communion most familiar to you and your people have special usefulness because they embody basic Christian teachings in a form designed to speak to the general mind of the church; and their repeated liturgical use gives the teaching power of

frequently renewed impression to associations built into them. Why not work out a brief series of sermon ideas based on one of these bodies of material?

For each sermon idea, clarify for yourself:

(a) an accurate statement of the meaning of the doctrine in your own words.

(b) some understanding of the experience from which it rose. This may well be clarified by probing your own experience and by concrete materials from your biographical reading.

(c) a text or biblical passage to give focus to the theme.

(d) a concise statement of some specific personal or social situation to which this doctrine speaks today.

After working on these ideas, you may be tempted to preach them at some early date. Do not spoil them by hurrying. It might prove more productive to put them away in your notebook for further reflection as a resource when you plan your preaching program for next year.

3. Using the discussion of "justification" (pp. 62-64) as a "sermon starter," try your hand at working out a sermon outline for the congregation you know best. Do not neglect to supplement this approach to the sermon with the worksheet process described in Chap. 2.

CHAPTER 4

Kerygma, Creed, and Christian Year

Who Has God's Point of View?

If valid doctrine serves so to distill experience that one man can point another to it or one generation share its insights with the next, it is still necessary to ask: Whose experience—tested by what standard? Do all experiences stand on a common level? If not, what gives some experiences authority to lay their claim upon us? One theologian recalls a dramatic moment when one of his seminary classmates interrupted a lecture to protest, "This may be true from our human standpoint, but from God's point of view—" Whereupon the professor broke in to inquire, "And who speaks from God's point of view?" [1] Who indeed? Among divergent understand-

[1] Claude H. Thompson, *Theology of the Kerygma* (Englewood Cliffs: Prentice-Hall, Inc., 1962), pp. 144 ff.

71

ings, how can the interpreter find that essential core of the message which makes it a saving word for a world off center?

In this quest, the semantic principle, "Find the referent," serves as a useful guide. A Word which God has given through Jesus Christ, not the formulations of church councils, provides the gospel's dynamic center—and that not in propositions but in encounter with him in whom "the Word became flesh and dwelt among us" (John 1:14). This living experience supplies faith's essential referent. The preacher cannot qualify as witness to the normative experience, but only as witness to the witnesses.[2] In the original testimony—the preaching of the apostles—a dependable body of concrete experience provides a centered message. Seeing clearly what comprises this testimony and how it relates to the modern preacher's discovery of living doctrine for a vital pulpit, enables him to deal more effectively with his all-important teaching task.

Referent for a Centered Gospel

C. H. Dodd has shown how the preaching (kerygma) of the apostles underlies the New Testament message. As a starting point for such a study, the sermons reported in the Acts of the Apostles provide a cross section of what early tradition remembered concerning the preaching of the first witnesses. Peter's sermons appear in suggestive outline in Acts 2:22-38; 3:12-26; 4:8-12; 5:29-32; 10:34-43. Sermons of Paul are reported in Acts 13:16-41; 17:22-31; 26:2-29. Paul briefly summarizes his own teaching in the salutation to the letter

[2] Cf. Jean Jacques von Allmen, *Preaching and Congregation* (Richmond: John Knox Press, 1962), p. 26.

to the Romans (1:1-6) and the introduction to his great chapter on the Resurrection (I Cor. 15:1-8).

After examining a considerable body of such material, Professor Dodd concluded that, despite differences in detail, it speaks with a unanimous voice concerning central matters. Whatever else might vary, these key items in the testimony appear in nearly all the preaching of the apostles: (a) "The age of fulfilment has dawned." (b) "This has taken place through the ministry, death, and resurrection of Jesus." (c) "By virtue of the resurrection, Jesus has been exalted at the right hand of God, as Messianic head of the new Israel." (d) "The Holy Spirit in the Church is the sign of Christ's present power and glory." (e) "The Messianic Age will shortly reach its consummation in the return of Christ." (f) "The kerygma always closes with an appeal for repentance, the offer of forgiveness and of the Holy Spirit, and the promise of 'salvation,' that is, of 'the life of the Age to Come,' to those who enter the elect community." [3]

Pursuing the matter further, Dodd discovered that this kerygma, not confined to a few passages reporting the sermons of the apostles, gives structure to the Gospels. Mark, for instance, begins—as does the preaching of the apostles—with the note of the dawning of the age of fulfillment: "As it is written in Isaiah the prophet" (1:2). Mark's stress on Jesus' baptism parallels that of the apostolic sermons as reported in Acts 10 and 13. The first half of the Gospel According to Mark presents in detail "Jesus of Nazareth, a man attested

---

[3] C. H. Dodd, *The Apostolic Preaching and Its Developments* (New York: Harper and Row, Publishers, 1936). Used by permission of Harper and Row, Publishers and Hodder and Stoughton Limited. Sentences quoted are excerpts from pp. 21-23.

to you by God with mighty works and wonders and signs which God did through him in your midst" (Acts 2:22); "how he went about doing good and healing all that were oppressed by the devil, for God was with him" (Acts 10:38) —characteristic emphases in the reported preaching of Peter. From its turning point—Mark 8:31—onward, the Gospel deals with the foreshadowings of the passion and with the details of the trial, crucifixion, and resurrection of Jesus, thus devoting a full half of the narrative to the items which receive most attention in the apostles' sermons.

From similar studies of the other Gospels, with like findings, Dodd concluded:

It is surely clear that the fourfold Gospel taken as a whole is an expression of the original apostolic Preaching. Of this the early Church was well aware. . . . We are not to think of the record in the Gospels as the ultimate raw material, out of which the Preaching was constructed. The kerygma is primary, and it acted as a preservative of the tradition which conveyed the facts. The nearer we are in the Gospels to the stuff of the kerygma, the nearer we are to the fountain-head of the tradition.[4]

Thus the work of a careful scholar of unimpeachable repute, confirmed with variations in detail but substantial agreement on the essential points by numerous other scholars, yields a core of original witness to concrete experience capable of providing a vital "operational referent" for a centered gospel.

In another of his summaries, Dodd gathers the recurring notes in the Pauline witness. Although, as he points out, not all of these items appear in every report of Paul's gospel

---

[4] *Ibid.*, p. 55.

proclamation, the total pattern runs consistently through his message.

> The prophecies are fulfilled, and the new Age is inaugurated by the coming of Christ.
>
> He was born of the seed of David.
>
> He died according to the Scriptures, to deliver us out of the present evil age.
>
> He was buried.
>
> He rose on the third day according to the Scriptures.
>
> He is exalted at the right hand of God, as Son of God and Lord of quick and dead.
>
> He will come again as Judge and Savior of men.[5]

This omits two important elements in the rounded message of the gospel as the New Testament declares it. There is no reference to the ministry of Jesus, with its teaching and healing, as Peter underscores it. Nor is there inclusion of the proclamation of the kingdom of God, which the Synoptic Gospels portray as the prominent emphasis in Jesus' own preaching. It should be noted that, although Paul gives relatively less prominence to Kingdom terminology than do the Synoptics, references to the kingdom of God do occur repeatedly in his letters. Even when he does not use this explicit phrase, the idea it represents is as central to his writing as to the Gospels. His constant emphasis on Christ as Lord carries the connotation of his reigning power. What affirmation of divine kingship could be loftier than Paul's "that at the name of Jesus every knee should bow, in heaven and on earth and under the earth, and every tongue confess that Jesus Christ is Lord,

---

[5] *Ibid.*, p. 17.

75

to the glory of God the Father" (Phil. 2:10-11)? God's reign through Christ, Paul declared, brings a new day for every man—indeed for all creation.[6] The Kingdom may not have a special place in the outline of Paul's preaching, but it is never far from his thinking.

This Pauline kerygma is so central to the Christian message that in the remaining chapters of our study we shall refer to it frequently. In the New Testament kerygma we have a concrete and dependable "operational referent" for a centered gospel, and in this outline of Paul's proclamation—supplemented at the two points we have noted—a useful and convenient summary of the kerygma.

God Known by His Acts

No semantic principle, however—important though it be —nor any utilitarian dictate of pulpit necessity can supply adequate ground for the choice of the central items in the preaching of the gospel. Unless the claim to centrality can be confirmed on theological grounds, its credentials are void. On these grounds the kerygma stands secure.

Biblical revelation unfolds through the medium of historic event. Evaluation is necessarily included, but the message remains at every point close to the field of human action. The Bible presents not a body of theory but a recital of deeds. Through the witnessing of these events "the penny drops, the light dawns," and there is a disclosure of life's meaning, of God's dealings with his children, the way of salvation. The Old Testament enacts an epic drama with a threefold *dramatis personae*: God, the nations, and Israel. The New Testament

* See p. 125.

likewise portrays events whose dramatic thread the kerygma serves to trace. Through them insight dawns, revelation is received, and God makes himself known.

In revelation so understood, valid theology comes to life. "A theology that is true to the basic character of the Christian religion is a theology of 'recital,' a theology that bases its knowledge of God and its descriptions of Him on what He has done in history." [7] In one of the most decisive statements of his commission to preach, Paul declares his conviction that "Christ did not send me to baptize but to preach the gospel, and not with eloquent wisdom, lest the cross of Christ be emptied of its power" (I Cor. 1:17). Here Paul not only contrasts theoretical statement—"eloquent wisdom"—on the one hand with specific event—"the cross of Christ"—on the other; he recognizes the sovereign dominance of event over theoretical statement. For this crucial statement of his understanding of his call to preach, Paul chooses among the available Greek verbs one which literally means "to bring or announce good news" as if doubly to underline his function as a reporter of events which carry the message.

Events so announced carry no merely antiquarian interest. It is not sufficient to know what transpired long ago; unless "the penny drops, the light dawns," and one sees himself in a new light which streams from these events, no revelation occurs. Rudolf Bultmann insists that biblical events become significant for us as we meet them in present reality and decision. As Francis Thompson put it, long before Bultmann, we know Jesus as our saving Lord when we see him

[7] Langdon Gilkey, Maker of Heaven and Earth (Garden City: Doubleday & Company, Inc., 1959), p. 289.

> . . . walking on the water
> Not of Gennesaret, but Thames! [8]

Resurrection matters to the modern man not as an event in the garden of Joseph of Arimathea but as a new dimension of reality in his own life. In the unfortunate word which has generated too much heat and too little light, to "demythologize" the New Testament accounts is so to penetrate mere recital of bygone events as to be confronted by a living Christ who calls us to present decision.

In the debate which Professor Bultmann precipitated, the key issue concerns the question whether the original events can themselves be regarded unimportant so long as the idea of them brings about the confrontation and decision. At this point, Dodd's stress on the events themselves, as they are set forth in the kerygma, comes to our assistance. Penetrate past recital to present encounter—"demythologize"—we must; make the events themselves unimportant—"dehistoricize"—we may not. The church's long insistence, despite baffling logical difficulties, that our Lord is both fully human and fully divine sheds light here. The living Christ can confront men in any age because, as fully divine, he transcends time and space. Yet the Christ who thus confronts us cannot be reduced to a projection of our religious sentiments because, as fully human, he possesses historical reality which resists our manipulations and constantly corrects our impressions of him.

In like manner, the kerygma at the heart of the New Testament message embodies that central core of memory which assures the integrity of the church's theology in a continued self-identity yet permits that identity to meet new situations

[8] From "In No Strange Land," by Francis Thompson.

with fresh understanding and creative adaptation. This is the function of memory in a man. Without his memories he could not be an integrated personality. Even in experiments with dogs, tricks played on memory induce breakdowns which rob an animal of its former identity. Build up associations between the ringing of a bell, response with a simple trick, and reward with food; then suddenly change the apparatus so that when the signal is given and the trick performed the result is not food but an electric shock; and after a series of repetitions of this complete violation of the dog's memory, he is no longer the same assured animal but a whimpering denial of his former self. For dog, man, or church, valid memory is crucial to identity. Yet creativity rests on ability to make fresh confrontations of new situations.

Resisting attempts to "dehistoricize" the message, the kerygma maintains its identity. Encouraging the penetration of mere recital of past events to arrive at present illumination and decision, the kerygma allows for growth and creativity. Thus it meets two prime requirements of a valid theology and supplies the "operational referent" for living doctrine in a vital pulpit.

Compass for Journeys in Scripture

What does it mean to say that the kerygma provides the living core of the message needed to save a world threatened by the loss of its true center? That the preacher must be endlessly repeating the story of the birth, death, resurrection, exaltation, and impending return of our Lord, with an appended appeal to repent and receive the new life by gift of the Holy Spirit? Must the modern preacher thus confine himself

79

to reproducing sermons on the standard outline of the preaching of the apostles?

Far from freeing the human spirit, this would imprison it.
To harden kerygma or creed into a formula to be strictly followed under all conditions is to deny faith. Such creedalism
attempts to walk by sight—certain positions established, crys-
tallized, no longer calling for or even permitting faith's daring
venture. It is the end of creativity, spiritual pioneering, salvation by faith. Creed and kerygma serve best as "travel reports
from previous voyagers on the sea of life." [9] Used as pointers
to the witness that carries greatest weight, keys to the understanding of where the focal centers of the biblical message can
be found, guides to the events which most dependably lead
to the moment of insight when "the penny drops" and "the
light dawns," the elements of the kerygma can serve the
preacher well.

Such use, without limiting his choice of texts or range of
subjects, will provide a principle of interpretation as he makes
his way through the Scriptures. To expound a Bible text is
not necessarily to preach the gospel. Textual preaching may
flog men's wills to keep the law, a task for which the diseased
will of man is no match. It may set forth that "wisdom"
which Paul explicitly renounced in favor of the good news of
the Cross. It may even provide pretext for culturally accommodated exhortations. As he makes his way through the Bible,
the preacher needs a guiding star to keep him on the track of
the gospel, lest he veer off course toward arid literalism in one
direction or a too vague attempt to read the Scriptures "in the
spirit of Jesus"—a "spirit" which, unless defined more pre-

[9] Nels F. S. Ferré, *The Finality of Faith* (New York: Harper and Row,
Publishers, 1963), p. 18.

cisely, too easily conforms to the predilections of the individual reader—in the other. Fixing attention on the key events
of God's act in Jesus Christ, the kerygma establishes the principle which distinguishes central matters from the literal but
secondary or the "spiritual" but too vague.

It has been well said that in the Apostles' Creed the church
supplies the minister with a compass which, wherever he
journeys through the Scriptures, points the direction to Bethlehem, Calvary, and Joseph's garden.[10] What is true of the
Creed is likewise true of the kerygma. Indeed the similarity
between kerygma and Apostles' Creed is obvious. Both begin
with a realization of the active God: "Maker of heaven and
earth," according to the Creed; so active in history that its
fulfillments in the coming of the new Age are his acts, according to the kerygma. Both continue with recital of the birth,
death, resurrection, exaltation, and expected coming of Jesus
Christ our Lord. Both end with the affirmation of new life
through the Holy Spirit—the kerygma by a call to repentance,
the Creed by promise of forgiveness which implies repentance.

Thus to preach the kerygma is not to be always setting
forth the successive articles of the Creed or the respective elements of the apostolic preaching. It is to discern the essential
gospel in any text by "sightings" from this compass which
points to the scenes of the nativity, crucifixion, and resurrection of our Lord; or, to change the figure, by taking seriously
the "travel reports" of those pioneer "voyagers," the apostles,
whose experience and witness most clarify the revelation for
us.

Thus to preach the kerygma is to find the most meaningful

[10] von Allmen, *op. cit.*, p. 24.

key for understanding the Christian year as a guide to a balanced presentation of the gospel. For the seasons of the year take their keynotes from the successive elements in the kerygma and their corresponding articles of the Creed. A study of any major lectionary of the church will reveal a doctrinal keynote running through the scripture lessons selected for any season. The preacher who lets this keynote establish the tonal range of his preaching, without explicitly harping on the indicated doctrine throughout the season, will be helped to establish balance and completeness in his message. Whether he follows the lectionary, season by season, or selects his texts in freer fashion, this doctrinal discernment will help him to find the "gospel" in the text and to keep the text within the circle of a more complete annual coverage of Christian truth.

Such an approach to the Christian year can be more meaningful than either a slavish following of the seasons out of dogged loyalty to liturgical custom or an attempt to make annual recapitulation of the life of Jesus. Under the doctrinal principle the traditional year "comes alive," opening depths of meaning which the recapitulation of the life of Jesus cannot yield. On the recapitulation theory, the Advent season, for instance, can lapse into sentimental expectations of the birth of "the baby Jesus"—a false note, since the baby Jesus was born, once for all, nineteen centuries ago. Though he is no longer to be expected in that way, the annual renewal of the church's hope of his coming as Judge and Savior and the sounding of the notes of his lordship of history and of personal fulfillment through him are forever needed. Thus the doctrinal approach to the Christian year satisfies the need for a sounder and more mature presentation of a centered gospel through which men meet the living Christ, with his promise and call to decision.

Doctrine in Unfolding Drama

Without in any sense implying that doctrines are confined within the bounds of given seasons, it will be helpful to note briefly how the respective seasons do provide channels for the preaching of the gospel as the kerygma brings it to focus.

Advent opens the annual drama of the mighty acts of God. "The prophecies are fulfilled," the kerygma announces, "and the new Age is inaugurated by the coming of Christ." Thus the Christian year dawns with acknowledgment of God's sovereign act as Lord of history. Expectancy sets the mood, but not the expectancy of Christmas—four weeks' celebration of that festival before its time. Expectancy is awakened, rather, by the mighty spectacle of the God who acts—whose comings are always imminent because he is history's Lord.

After an Advent season spent with these commanding realities, Christmas sounds its proper stress on the birth of our Lord, unspoiled by a sentimental season of "preparation for Christmas." "He was born of the seed of David," declares the kerygma; and the Creed affirms faith in "Jesus Christ, [God's] only Son our Lord; who was conceived by the Holy Spirit, born of the Virgin Mary." All great Christian preaching stems from this high Christology. "The Word became flesh and dwelt among us." (John 1:14.) "God was in Christ reconciling the world to himself." (II Cor. 5:19.) "Who, though he was in the form of God, did not count equality with God a thing to be grasped, but emptied himself, taking the form of a servant, being born in the likeness of men."

(Phil. 2:6-7.) Such declarations bind the faith of the New Testament into living unity. Unless this doctrine of God's act in a Christ fully divine and fully human is so realistically explored that men are helped to believe it deeply, the Crucifixion is reduced to another martyrdom, the Resurrection to fantasy. Preaching that passes through Christmastide without clear and vital teaching of this doctrine signally fails in its high opportunity.

January 6, with the traditional gospel of the visit of the Wise Men and its note of the revelation of Christ to the Gentiles, brings the festival of Epiphany. As the term implies, this opens the season of the *unveiling* or *revelation* of God in Christ. A familiar Epiphany epistle affirms: "For it is the God who said, 'Let light shine out of darkness,' who has shone in our hearts to give the light of the knowledge of the glory of God in the face of Christ." (II Cor. 4:6.) This unveiling of God's nature through the character of Christ safeguards a faith that maintains ethical as well as mystical continuity with Jesus. The revelation of God in Christ to the Gentiles suggests the missionary outreach of the faith, calls for a strong missions note in preaching, and leads to the application of the gospel to widening circles of life, including interfaith understanding, as Brotherhood Sunday—falling in this season —invites, and a recognition of human dignity across racial lines, as Race Relations Sunday demands.

Lent echoes to the kerygma's proclamation: "He died according to the Scriptures, to deliver us out of the present evil age. He was buried." He "suffered under Pontius Pilate, was crucified, dead and buried," the Creed affirms. Overshadowed by the Cross, Lent is preeminently the season of the Atonement. The disciplines of the Cross as Jesus lived with them, his challenge to each disciple to take up his cross and follow him, the deeper meaning of the Cross in the reconciliation of rebellious humanity to a loving God—these dominate the message of Lent. In its traditional first Sunday gospel, the story of the wilderness temptations, Jesus made the basic decisions that led to the Cross. Stewardship Sunday, often observed on the third or fourth Sunday of Lent, views our life in all its practical dimensions under this claim. Passion Sunday, Palm Sunday, and Good Friday bring this message to dramatic climax.

Eastertide offers seven Sundays in which to sustain the kerygma's cry of victory: "He rose on the third day according to the Scriptures." Easter day cannot probe the depths of the gospel of the Resurrection—the wonder of God's victory over evil; Christ's eternal lordship; life everlasting confronting our mortality and assuring us that all graves open toward God's heaven; and the "power of an endless life" as, risen with him, we seek those things which are above. Only a full use of the seven Sundays of Eastertide can explore these vital themes.

On the eve of Pentecost comes the short season of Ascensiontide, of which the kerygma says, "He is exalted at the right hand of God, as Son of God and Lord of quick and dead." Many ministers remain silent concerning this doctrine, embarrassed by alleged space connotations of its language. In an age when astronomy makes this imagery seem ridiculous, it is necessary to stress again the semantic principle which calls for peering beyond words to the experiences they attempt to express. No longer encountered in such bodily appearances as the Resurrection message portrayed, no longer bound to Palestinian localities, Christ comes to multitudes of men and women in widely separated times and places. We can know him as "our eternal contemporary," ever infinitely above us in his lordship, ever near in a companionship transcending time and space. All this the gospel of the Ascension gathers in a graphic picture. As a memorable preacher of the last generation declared, we need to discover anew that the ascension of Christ, not the "descent of man," gives the key to life's meaning.[11]

Pentecost invites preaching on the Third Article of the Creed, associating the Holy Spirit with the church, the communion of saints, forgiveness, resurrection, and life everlasting. Though they are omitted from Dodd's summary of the Pauline kerygma, these doctrines were prominent in Paul's teaching. Professor Dodd's own résumé of the fuller apostolic preaching reminds us that "the kerygma always closes with an appeal for repentance, the offer of forgiveness and of the Holy Spirit, and the promise of 'salvation,' that is, of 'the life of the Age to come,' to those who enter the elect community." With Pentecost's celebration of the gift of the Holy Spirit, the first half of the Christian year is completed and the mighty saving acts of God through Jesus Christ have passed in review. Trinity Sunday then gathers this richly varied experience of God—as Creator, Redeemer, Sanctifying Spirit—into a unified view of his one reality, leading into the remaining half-year, the semester of the church sent forth with this glorious

---

[11] Cf. "He Ascended into Heaven," a sermon for Ascensiontide by G. A. Studdert-Kennedy, in *Master Sermons Through the Ages*, ed. William Alan Sadler, Jr. (New York: Harper and Row, Publishers, 1963), pp. 199 ff.

gospel to proclaim the message that can restore the world to
its lost center.

The Festival of Christ the King, on the last Sunday in
August, opens the season of Kingdomtide, which extends
through the weeks that remain until Advent and the recurring
cycle of a new year. In this closing season the whole commanding panoply of kerygmatic teaching is brought to bear on
all the widening relationships of life: personal allegiance to
Christ, suggested by the Festival of Christ the King; industrial
relations, suggested by Labor Sunday; the life of the mind,
suggested by the reopening of schools; the special claims of
Christian education, suggested by Church School Rally Day;
the ecumenical unity of the church, suggested by World
Communion Sunday; order among nations under law, suggested by World Order Sunday; "the crown rights of the Redeemer" within his church, suggested by Reformation Sunday; our unbroken fellowship with all the living and the dead
who are in Christ, suggested by All Saints Day; the claims of
human need upon Christian stewardship, suggested by the
season of Community Fund campaigns in most cities and
towns; and the loving response of his disciples and subjects,
suggested by Thanksgiving Day. Thus the message of the kingdom of God, a dominant note of the New Testament and the
theme of the great parables, finds its assured place in the
drama of the Christian year.

For drama it is, as playwright Dorothy Sayers has reminded
us. Concerning her play, The Zeal of Thy House, Miss Sayers
remarks that the critics liked it as drama but objected that it
included too much Christian dogma. But "the dogma *is* the
drama," she retorted. And they are wrong who suppose that

Christianity is some common denominator of genteel respectability to which the doctrines which take seriously such matters as the kerygma sets forth are secondary. Such a religion makes itself believable by reduction to such dullness that it matters little whether anyone believes it or not. A faith declared in the full dramatic claim of its great doctrines may present a difficult challenge to the mind, but *dull* it never can be. In the full sweep of its teaching, men see that it matters so much that believers and unbelievers alike can wish it to be true.[12]

Bringing the preacher over these varied routes to the living heart of the gospel, the kerygma assures variety and orderly progress in the message.

There is law and there is gospel, and there is gospel in law and law in gospel. There are the rocky steeps of Sinai and the green pastures of Galilee, there are parables by the lake and the sword piercing through the soul on the way to Calvary. Always to be denouncing, always to be pleading, always to be in the depths or in the heights, always to be using the moral whip or always to be supposing that nothing is involved except 'my yoke is easy,' is just to miss the one great thing in life that is worth preaching about, all its heights and its depth.[13]

To the exploration of this endlessly varied, constantly commanding gospel we now turn. The remaining chapters of this book seek to suggest something of the preaching message of each of the key declarations of the kerygma.

[12] Dorothy L. Sayers, *Creed or Chaos?* (New York: Harcourt, Brace and Company, 1949), pp. 21, 23 ff.

[13] John Oman, *Concerning the Ministry* (New York: Harper & Brothers, 1937), p. 69; (Paper ed.; Richmond: John Knox Press, 1963).

FOR FURTHER STUDY

1. Beyond the brief summary of C. H. Dodd's *The Apostolic Preaching and Its Developments* (New York: Harper and Row, Publishers, 1936) given in the foregoing discussion, a firsthand study of this important book will be rewarding. *Theology of the Kerygma*, by Claude H. Thompson (Englewood Cliffs: Prentice-Hall, Inc., 1962), and *God Who Redeems*, by Eric H. Wahlstrom (Philadelphia: Fortress Press, 1962), offer significant recent contributions to the discussion of biblical theology. On the debate occasioned by the work of Rudolf Bultmann, a symposium edited by Carl E. Braaten and Roy A. Harrisville under the title, *Kerygma and History* (Nashville: Abingdon Press, 1962), is probably the most useful summary. Though it is not easy reading, the preacher will find it informative and helpful.

The best single guide to the liturgical year is *Preaching the Christian Year*, edited by Howard Albert Johnson (New York: Charles Scribner's Sons, 1957). Lectionaries used in our study are *The Book of Common Prayer* of the Protestant Episcopal Church, *The Book of Common Worship* of the Presbyterian Church (U.S.A.), *The Book of Worship* of The Methodist Church, 1945; and, for the lectionary of the Lutheran churches, the most useful source for the minister of another denomination is found in John W. Doberstein's excellent *Minister's Prayer Book* (Philadelphia: Fortress Press, 1959).

2. Have you begun a notebook related to your preaching plan for next year? Now is the time to take a further step in the project. On several sheets of paper—to allow space to scratch out old entries and make new ones as your thought develops—write the dates of the Sundays of the year, indicating the beginning of each liturgical season. Suggestions for this phase of your planning are found on p. 44. With your notebook set up in this fashion, you are now prepared to work at your preaching plan along two con-

verging lines: beginning with Bible studies and working toward their place in the calendar, and starting with the needs and emphases of the seasons and working back toward biblical and doctrinal sources. The studies growing out of the remaining chapters of this book will prove doubly fruitful if you engage in such a planning project as you proceed.

🌷

CHAPTER 5

Expecting
History's Lord to Come

"The Word Is with Men"?

When Christians confess, "I believe in God, the
Father Almighty, Maker of heaven and earth," they speak of
no withdrawn, aloof Deity but of a God who comes. The
Creed affirms not only that he made the world but that he
came in Jesus Christ our Lord and "shall come to judge the
quick and the dead." Our faith finds voice in the lyric cry of
the psalmist:

> Let the hills sing for joy together
> before the Lord, for he comes
> to rule the earth.
> —Ps. 98:8-9a

91

With this conviction that he is the God who comes, the preaching of Paul began and ended. "The prophecies are fulfilled, and the new Age is inaugurated by the coming of Christ"—so, as C. H. Dodd reports it, the Pauline kerygma opens. "He will come again as Judge and Savior of men" [1]— so it concludes. He is history's Lord. We who put our trust in him live in perpetual expectation, between the times of his coming.

This faith, by no means universal among men of goodwill who influence contemporary society, has become a battle line. There is a sense of shock as the closing words of John Steinbeck's Nobel Prize acceptance speech paraphrase a classic Christian affirmation: "In the end is the word, and the word is man, and the word is with men." So the honored novelist issued a needed moral challenge. He had been paying tribute to Alfred Nobel, who, perceiving that his discovery of high explosives could be either a boon or an unprecedented curse, set out to erect defenses against the dread potential. The crucial decision, he saw, lay with the human spirit as men decided what to do with the power placed in their hands. Concerning nuclear-age choices far more crucial, Steinbeck was right to underscore Nobel's summons to the spirit of man.

But is this the final word? Is man's the only word? Many a modern answers, "Yes! Man, and only man, must determine history's outcome." In Steinbeck's judgment:

Having taken God-like power, we must seek in ourselves for the responsibility and the wisdom we once prayed some deity might

[1] Dodd, op. cit., p. 17. Italics added.

have. Man himself has become our greatest hazard and our only hope. So that today, St. John the Apostle may well be paraphrased:

In the end is the word, and the word is man, and the word is *with* men.[2]

To this assertion the Christian replies: "You may not leave out of account the God who comes!" The World Council of Churches, calling men to struggle with the monumental tasks of this time, underscores this factor.

We are not sufficient for these things. But Christ is sufficient. We do not know what is coming to us. But we know Who is coming. It is He who meets us every day and who will meet us at the end—Jesus Christ our Lord.

Therefore we say to you: "Rejoice in hope." [3]

These words echo the faith that sustained much of the most heroic service amid the hopelessness that blanketed Europe after World War II. Inscribed on the wall of a thrice-bombed hospital, it spoke in words that strengthened the deaconess staff through all hazards: "We do not know what is coming, but we know who is coming—Christ."

Let that declaration ring in our hearts, challenge and sustain our deeds, meet today's emergent issues in our pulpits. God, who acted decisively in history, is its Lord who will act. We live in expectation of his coming.

[2] Nobel Prize acceptance speech by John Steinbeck, delivered in Stockholm, December 10, 1962, as published in a supplement to the Book-of-the-Month Club *News*.

[3] *The Evanston Report*, The Second Assembly of the World Council of Churches, 1954, ed. W. A. Visser't Hooft (New York: Harper and Row, Publishers, 1955), p. 3.

Responsible Men Meet Decisive God

Those who rally to this faith raise a battle standard bearing the watchword: History lies within God's control. In the biblical view, events transpire on a field of continuous interaction between men, who bear responsibility for their choices, and God, who uses even the unwilling and rebellious to effect his ends.

Over Scripture's vast stage troop those in whom this interaction is seen at work. Joseph, looking back over his brothers' treachery and the outcome to which it led, sees another hand. "So it was not you who sent me here, but God," he tells his forgiven brothers. "You meant evil against me; but God meant it for good." (Gen. 45:8; 50:20.) To a cruel Pharaoh, God sends Moses to say: "For this purpose have I let you live, to show you my power, so that my name may be declared throughout all the earth." (Exod. 9:16.) He prompts Isaiah to characterize the conqueror used to effect God's purifying purpose as "Assyria, the rod of my anger" (Isa. 10:5), though the Assyrian dreams of no service to the Lord:

> He does not so intend,
> and his mind does not so think;
> but it is in his mind to destroy,
> and to cut off nations not a few.
> —Isa. 10:7

Yet, declares Isaiah, God has the last word: "When the Lord has finished all his work on Mount Zion and on Jerusalem he will punish the arrogant boasting of the king of Assyria and his haughty pride" (10:12). To the imperious Assyrian God says:

> Shall the axe vaunt itself over him who
>   hews with it,
> or the saw magnify itself against him
>   who wields it?
>
> —Isa. 10:15

With the same prophetic view, Jeremiah sees Nebuchadrezzar as invincible only until the divine purpose is accomplished.

Turning to the New Testament, one sees the unmistakably sinful choices of men. Judas betrays his Lord, the Temple authorities demand his death, Pilate temporizes and capitulates, and the soldiers implement the evil with instruments of brutality—cross, hammer and spikes, the thrust of a spear. But the cross, tool of man's worst, becomes the agency of God's best. In a single line of his sermon at Pentecost, Peter portrays the interaction of men with an overriding God: "This Jesus, delivered up according to the definite plan and foreknowledge of God, you crucified and killed by the hands of lawless men" (Acts 2:23).[4] So runs the sustained insight of the Bible. Men are responsible for their choices, but God uses their acts to effect his own purpose as Lord of history.

To us, who must walk by faith and not by sight, this truth remains at issue because God's fulfillments are far from simple and direct. A long road of deferment lies between the promise to Abraham and its fulfillment in Christ. Endless vigils follow the prophecies of hope in the Exile and the church's expectancy of our Lord's return. Though Paul cites events in Christ's life and ministry as occurring "according to the Scriptures," the fulfillments do not vindicate specific sayings; but

[4] Cf. Eric H. Wahlstrom, *God Who Redeems* (Philadelphia: Fortress Press, 1962), pp. 47-69.

in the long view Christ completes the central message that threads its way through the Old Testament.

When Jesus told his Nazareth neighbors, "Today this scripture has been fulfilled in your hearing" (Luke 4:21), he did not, there and then, release captives, restore sight to the blind, liberate the oppressed. No description of the moment, this was an interpretation of his mission, a frontispiece to the gospel. In this deeper, more lasting sense the wistful hope of Israel had been realized, the new age had begun. Yet the need for release, recovering of sight, liberation of the oppressed is still with us. God, who has acted and will act, calls us to responsible participation.

New Testament Greek, having access to two words for time where we must make do with one, facilitates the expression of this biblical view of history. Chronos designates time as duration—calendar time, clock time, root of our "chronology," "chronic," "chronometer." But kairos presents another dimension of time—a prepared hour of destiny and decision, somewhat as we say "the time is ripe," "the time is propitious," "the time is out of joint." The English historian G. M. Trevelyan gives an example of kairos, time in this more decisive sense, in the historic setting of Shakespeare's life. The peculiar genius of the poet is beyond question; no conspiracy of external forces could account for his accomplishments— his enrichment of the human mind, his ennoblement of men's spirits, his impact on language and literature through centuries to follow. Yet a special good fortune inhered in the coming of exactly this personality of genius at exactly this hour when the growth of the thought, life, and speech of Britain and the development of the London theater made his achievements possible. Shakespeare was responsible, yet forces

96

beyond his command were at work. From the interaction of
the poet with his time (*kairos*) the achievements emerged. In
some such manner, faith affirms, God works in the affairs of
men.

Our generation is not without examples. *Time* magazine
annually selects a "Man of the Year" who, in the opinion of
Time's editors, "dominated the news that year and left an
indelible mark—for good or ill—on history." [5] The choice has
fallen on both saints and despots—Schweitzer, Gandhi, Stal-
in, Hitler, Martin Luther King, Pope John XXIII—yet, looking back over the years, it grows apparent that, decisive as
such figures were, events did not turn out according to their
plans. Whoever might be man of the year, setting his mark
on events, the pattern of history itself lay in the hand of a
higher Sovereign. Of affairs so ordered the World Council of
Churches spoke truly: "We do not know what is coming to
us. But we know Who is coming. It is He who meets us every
day and who will meet us at the end."

Between "Already" and "Not Yet"

If those who live by this faith raise as their first battle
standard one which proclaims: History lies within God's control, their second bears the device: We live by faith "between
the times." In Karl Barth's dramatic terms, we do not live
between birth and death but between baptism and the Lord's
Supper—between his coming to us first in the sacrament that
bound us to him, and his coming again in the sacrament that
renews our life. [6] With an even more radical sense of living

[5] *Time*, Jan. 4, 1963, p. 11.
[6] *God in Action* (Great Neck, N. Y.: Round Table Press, 1963), p. 111.

in sustained expectancy, Christians employ the imagery of our Lord's first and second comings.

Paul Tillich, using this language, speaks of a twofold sense in which Jesus is the "end" of history. He is its end because he brings the fulfillment of its aim. Thus in his first coming he brought into view a new order of life—in Tillich's term, "the New Being." But he is history's end in another sense. In him our existence in "estrangement, conflicts, self-destruction" is brought to a finish.[7] Those bound to him in faith's compact find an inner peace which brings estrangement to a full stop.

Because this second coming of the Lord has not yet occurred for a lost world, we live in an historical predicament full of distortions and ambiguities, between the "already" of his first coming and the "not yet" of the second. When Christians speak not of some fuller development in the evolution of man but of our Lord's second coming, they safeguard an important truth: Whatever comes as a further fulfillment of our life must not contradict or distort what has come to us in Christ. He has no successor. No such faith as the Baha'i syncretism, which would go beyond Christ to some fuller knowledge of God and his salvation, can avail. When life comes to us in richer measure than we have known, he will proffer the gift. To accept what departs from or professes to go beyond him is to accept less than the best. New developments do not test him; he tests them. Yet we, who know that we have not yet received from him all that he has to offer, live in the tension between "already" and "not yet."[8]

Temptations are numerous to flee this tension, to act as if Christ did have a successor. Shortcuts to fulfillment bid for

[7] *Op. cit.*, II, 119 ff.
[8] *Ibid.*, pp. 163 ff.

our allegiance, making their appeal to one or another of such factors, essential to meaning in our life, as the hope of the fulfillment of our deepest needs, the vision of an intelligible and purposeful order of significance in which we can take our part, or some promise of inner health and unity. Three would-be "successors" to Christ as Lord of life have come upon the scene in our time. Technical science has given rise to "scientism" with its rosy promise that science can fulfill our deepest needs. The dream of some automatic progress in history, at one extreme, or the Marxian dogma of a dialectic of history, at the other, has inspired men to believe they have found the key to an understandable and purposeful order in which they can play their part. Psychoanalysis has been, for many, the source of the promise of inner health and unity.[9] But such partial, often erroneous, fulfillments leave their devotees frustrated and betrayed. Christ has no successor.

So we live by faith "between the times." In a luminous passage in one of his sermons, John Baillie calls to remembrance winter evenings of blackout during World War II in which he reread a good many books growing out of the previous war. One of them posed the questions: Who really won the war for us? What kind of man was he? Discussion led to the answer that "he was a plain man awake all night in a ditch." Professor Baillie adds, as comment, a confession of faith: "Is that not the kind of man who by the grace of God will always win the battle of life—a plain man on the watch?"[10] Such a man lives as Christians must, in the tension

[9] Cf. Gilkey, op. cit., pp. 153 ff.
[10] John Baillie, *Christian Devotion* (New York: Charles Scribner's Sons, 1962), p. 60.

"between the times," expecting to meet history's Lord at any moment.

Crisis of Judgment and Hope

As the battle standards gather around this faith, one proclaims: History lies within God's control; another: We live by faith "between the times"; and blazoned on a third flames the conviction: We live in the crisis of judgment and hope.

For between "already" and "not yet" Christians occupy an eternal present. They cherish a heritage from the yesterdays conveyed to them through the Bible and the heroic memories of the church; yet when they read these historic records, it is not the *past* they encounter but the living present. One theologian's quaint phrase, "the isness of the was," lays its claim on the preacher. For, as preacher, he deals with biblical material not to make scholarly reconstruction of a bygone day but to bring men face to face with a living issue and a living God. "The isness of the was" presents its claim to every man. Each man of our time lives as near the Fall as did Moses, for *we* are the fallen creatures. Each stands in just such relation to the Resurrection as did Peter and Paul, for our risen Lord comes also to us. We cherish our biblical heritage wrongly if we look *back* to it, rightly if through it we face more realistically the ultimate issues in the living present.[11]

Not only heritage but hope conditions the Christian. He does not so much strain toward a distant future as encounter each living present under a light shed on it by his expectation of God's action. Judgment confronts him at every turn. Though we cannot trace its contours in detail, we cannot

[11] Cf. Thompson, *op. cit.*, pp. 23-28.

escape the evidences of its outcroppings at least at some points in the history of nations and in our personal affairs. When we presume to know more about God's judgments than is given to mortals to understand, we grow self-righteous or take it upon ourselves to mete out judgment in God's behalf. What a trial of woe and spiritual damnation this sin leaves in its wake! Judgment is God's business, not to be taken into our hands. Yet guilt and retribution constantly recur in human affairs, as conscience and history's gigantic reckonings bear witness.

For those who trust a God who saves, judgment is accompanied by hope. One of the traditional lessons for Advent (Isa. 35) portrays this truth. Strength for the living present vibrates in Isaiah's word:

> Say to those who are of a fearful heart,
> "Be strong, fear not!"
> —Vs. 4

Despite all dangers, men face the testing hour unafraid, secure in their expectancy of God's coming:

> Behold, your God
> will come with vengeance,
> with the recompense of God.
> He will come and save you.
> —Vs. 4

These words follow a scene of devastation (Isa. 31) as stark as any that haunts the dreams of atomic scientists today. Such, the prophet declares, is the judgment of God; such is his vengeance. Living by this faith, we need not take vengeance

101

in our own hands. "Beloved, never avenge yourselves," writes Paul, "but leave it to the wrath of God; for it is written, 'Vengeance is mine, I will repay, says the Lord.' " (Rom. 12: 19.) Dare we, who live by faith in a God who comes, live by that rule in such a world as this? Throughout this bloody century, our vengeance has bathed the world in tears. Can we learn to trust his rule for the crucial decisions amidst cold war, race tensions, personal entanglements?

Isaiah proclaims this as the only way. Under the bitter displacements of his time he lifted the assurance:

> Behold, your God will come
> . . . and save you
> . . . and the ransomed of the Lord shall return.
> —Isa. 35:4, 10

Such faith in "the isness of the shall be" has brought strength to men in hopeless situations in our day. In postwar years, when Europe was dotted with drab refugee camps peopled with the homeless who sank ever deeper in despair, the church built such refugee villages as the beautiful Freiheim, near Lübeck, hardly more than a stone's throw from the bristling barbed wire of the Iron Curtain frontier, where refugees found hope reborn and life renewed. Far from supine and passive in their expectation of God's coming, these Christians were given vitality that made them creative centers of saving action. There is judgment and there is hope, and we live at the crucial point of their meeting.

"Then the eyes of the blind shall be opened." (Isa. 35:5.) Living with our heritage as if it were only a record of the past, and with our hope as if it were nothing but a dream of the future, we are blind to the ever-present crisis of judgment and hope. Isaiah's promise speaks to our need.

When the Bells Ring on Sunday

In the light of this faith the preaching task is clear. Among men informed and guided by goodwill, who build their lives on the supposition that in every decision the last word lies with men, we lift an embattled and challenging faith that history, as continual interaction between responsible men and the God who comes, bends finally to his control. We call men to an awareness that they live "between the times" and that hope lies not in flight from the tensions of such a life— flight which can end only in frustration and destruction—but in faith's watchfulness. We seek the opening of the eyes of the blind, that they may see the crisis of judgment and hope in which we live. When the bells ring at eleven o'clock on Sunday morning, they call the servant of the Word to precipitate that crisis.

This is no seasonal truth. Never untimely in the Christian pulpit, it is given an assured place in the Christian year as the keynote of the Advent message. The liturgies of the Episcopal, Lutheran, and Presbyterian churches choose the same epistles for these four Sundays:

Advent Sunday	— Rom. 13:11-14
Second Sunday	— Rom. 15:4-13
Third Sunday	— I Cor. 4:1-5
Fourth Sunday	— Phil. 4:4-8

A study of these lessons in the light of the doctrine of the God who comes can lead to vital preaching.

The lesson for Advent Sunday calls us, who live in perpetual crisis at the meeting point of judgment and hope, to awakened expectancy:

Besides this you know what hour it is, how it is full time now for you to wake from sleep. For salvation is nearer to us now than when we first believed; the night is far gone, the day is at hand. Let us then cast off the works of darkness and put on the armor of light.

—Rom. 13:11-12

Does not the juxtaposition of theme and text call the preacher to double analysis in the light of his own time and place, from which a burning message can emerge as God guides him to speak to the needs of his own people?

The keynote of the lesson for Universal Bible Sunday, second Sunday in Advent, is sounded in its opening verse: "For whatever was written in former days was written for our instruction, that by steadfastness and by the encouragement of the scriptures we might have hope" (Rom. 15:4). How magnificently this brings together the heritage, the hope, and the crucial present, as the scriptures give them life for those who live in this sense of God's ever-impending coming! A study of the remaining verses of the lesson will supply abundant detail for helpful preaching on this theme.

The note of judgment rings clearly in the lessons for the third Sunday in Advent. Witness this excerpt:

But with me it is a very small thing that I should be judged by you or by any human court. I do not even judge myself. I am not aware of anything against myself, but I am not thereby acquitted. It is the Lord who judges me. Therefore do not pronounce judgment before the time, before the Lord comes, who will bring to light the things now hidden in darkness and will disclose the purposes of the heart.

—I Cor. 4:3-5

How powerfully this speaks of: (a) the God who comes to judge us, (b) the folly of our human judgments of one another, (c) the independence with which we dare follow our convictions despite the adverse judgments of others, (d) the need of each of us to turn from our shallow, self-justifying judgments to faith's acceptance of the judgment of God.

On the Sunday before Christmas, the Advent note of hope receives the full and grateful attention it deserves: "The Lord is at hand" (Phil. 4:5). The God who comes is at our door! As the lesson makes clear, knowing this we (a) rejoice, (b) have no anxiety, (c) are kept in God's peace.

One of the most beautiful of the traditional Advent lessons (Isa. 52:7-10) puts the season's theme in a picture:

> How beautiful upon the mountains
> are the feet of him who brings good
> tidings,
> who publishes peace, who brings good
> tidings of good,
> who publishes salvation,
> who says to Zion, "Your God reigns."
>
> —Vs. 7

So reads the opening verse, telling helpless exiles of a God who comes, so that despite all appearances to the contrary, he holds history in his control. "Your God reigns."

The picture suggests a deep mountain valley at dawn. Have you been in such a place? Around you the night lingered, the darkness penetrated only by the faint gray that filtered through. But looking up, you saw the mountaintop bathed in the gold of a sunrise that had not yet reached your valley. Its beauty sang "the song of a new dawn waking." So, said the prophet of the Exile, in the dark night the mountaintops are already aglow with the rays of the new day of God's coming. That strengthened the exiles. It brings creative, saving hope to Christians in every dark time. In a world of disorder it strengthens the hands of those who give allegiance to order under law through the United Nations. In the anarchy of an arms race it speaks renewed strength to those who venture to struggle for disarmament. The promise that "all the ends of the earth shall see the salvation of our God" comes as the needed word of hope to members of oppressed races, to those who give themselves to world missions, and to the last desperate man who feels, "I am beyond hope."

Here is a faith to live by, ever renewed in expectancy that history's Lord will come. "We do not know what is coming to us. But we know Who is coming. It is He who meets us every day and who will meet us at the end—Jesus Christ our Lord."

FOR FURTHER STUDY

1. Among the numerous books dealing with the philosophy of history, special relevance for the preacher will be found in *Christianity and History*, by Herbert Butterfield (Paper ed.; New York: Charles Scribner's Sons, 1950), and *Christ and History*, by George A. Buttrick (Nashville: Abingdon Press, 1963). For the relation of the material to the Advent season, the reader is referred to the lectionaries and again to Johnson's *Preaching the Christian Year*.

2. You may wish to begin developing a series of sermon ideas around the epistles cited on p. 103. Germs of "sermon starters" for the four sermons of such a series will be found on pp. 103-6. Why not begin work on them in your notebook of plans for next year?

3. Allowing these four ideas time to germinate, perhaps you might take some other aspect of the theme developed in this chapter as the basis for a sermon outline to be brought to maturity for earlier use: God's sovereignty in history (pp. 94-97), or the call to live on the watch (pp. 97-100), or the crisis of judgment and hope (pp. 100-103), or the suggested exposition of Isa. 52:7-10 (pp. 105-6).

❦

CHAPTER 6

Preaching
The Good News of Incarnation

Where the Interpreter Finds Power

Nothing is more central to the gospel than the question: Who is Jesus? Both outside and within the church, this issue troubles earnest souls. Amid turmoil and suffering, one church member wrote: "My only certainty is that I believe in Jesus with all my heart, soul, mind, and strength. I say 'only in Jesus' because sometimes I feel that he was overwhelmed by both the evil of men and by a cruel higher power that required the Crucifixion." Possessing devotion to Jesus, the writer of these words had much. Yet the question, "Who is Jesus?" remains crucial. Was he "overwhelmed by both the evil of men and by a cruel higher power"? Was he a lonely Prometheus, not chained to a rock but nailed to a cross by the decree of a God who stood against him?

The answer colors the whole approach to life. To sharpen

the difference, move into geographic areas not deeply influenced by a Christ who, far from being "overwhelmed by a
cruel higher power," comes as God's ultimate expression. A
traveler brings back a report of coolies going on with their
work on shipboard after seeing one of their number fall into
the waves. That they substituted wry jokes for rescue attempts, the report added, evidenced no peculiar inhumanity
among them. It stemmed rather from their belief that to save
another from drowning is to interfere with fate. Should the
rescued sustain injury, the rescuer would incur lifelong responsibility. Having robbed fate of its prey, he must meet the
heavy costs of his meddling.[1] The incident and its explanation
highlight the change in social climate which accompanies
passage from faith in the Father of Jesus Christ to belief in
the gods of fate.

Who, then, is Jesus? Christianity's centered gospel replies
that he was a man—as fully human as any man can be—but
he was no overwhelmed struggler against a higher power, for
in him God himself came to us. Proclaiming that "he was
born of the seed of David," the kerygma speaks of his full
humanity, entering our life through the channel of birth,
taking his place in the historic sequence of a national and
family line with all its social, cultural, religious heritage. But
the kerygma makes this declaration in the context of the announcement that it is *God* who comes in him: "The

---

[1] Helmut Thielicke, Voyage to the Far East (Philadelphia: Fortress Press,
1962), p. 22. Disturbing parallels stain the American scene. The thirty-eight
apartment dwellers in Queens, New York, who for half an hour watched three
separate stabbing attacks which took the life of a young woman, without
moving to aid her or to call the police, present only the most dramatic of
numerous similar episodes. Is it mere coincidence that such symptoms appear
in a period so secularized that some thoughtful observers call it "post-Chris-
tian"?

prophecies are fulfilled, and the new Age is inaugurated by the coming of Christ. . . . He will come again as Judge and Savior of men."

We take our orientation toward life, our fellowmen, and ourselves from the fixed star of our faith that God came to us in Jesus. Over this fulcrum our understanding of the Crucifixion swings toward belief either in atonement or in another deed of barbaric depravity, of the Resurrection toward hope or incredulity and despair, of the call to go into all the world and make disciples toward a saving crusade or another dream of overreaching ambition, and of our Lord's reported presence with the faithful toward stark reality or sheer wish-fulfillment. Here we stand at the strategic center for preaching, because here we are brought to life's central question.

The Word Became Flesh—Not Concept

Far more than pragmatic usefulness, this faith in the good news of the Incarnation offers the truest reading of the meaning of Jesus' life and of our own existence.

Jesus himself did not believe he stood alone against a cruel higher power. As the night of opposition closed around him, he foresaw a time when all men would turn against him; yet he remained confident that he would wage no solitary battle. "The hour is coming," he said, "indeed it has come, when you will be scattered, every man to his home, and will leave me alone; yet I am not alone, for the Father is with me." (John 16:32.) Far from dreading the oppression of "a cruel higher power," he said: "I and the Father are one" (John 10:30). To Philip's question in the Upper Room, he replied: "He who has seen me has seen the Father; how can you say, 'Show us the Father'?" (John 14:9). In this language peculiar

110

to the Fourth Gospel he makes only a little more emphatic what lies implicit in the Synoptics. The Christ of Matthew, Mark, and Luke declares that those who build on his words build on rock; he invites men to follow him at cost of a cross; he bids for allegiance above all, whether it be the dear ties of family or one's own life; he shows himself at once the humblest of men—washing his disciples' feet, asking, "Why do you call me good?"—and the most exalted—promising to save the lost, commissioning his disciples to a worldwide mission in his name. All this rests upon the assumption that he is no lone, overwhelmed man but that in him we meet God.

Subsequent experience with him, endlessly repeated, underscores his belief about himself. One who, like the writer of the letter we have quoted, begins by believing "only in Jesus . . . with all my heart, soul, mind, and strength" can follow that road to vital communion with God. Over this route so many have come to full and transforming faith that with confidence one can say to such perplexed persons: Continue along the path you have begun. Believing in Jesus, meet him daily in the gospel records, seeking not only to understand him but to obey his directives for your own outlook and conduct. A day will come when you will realize whom you are meeting. It is not a *doctrine* we trust, but a Person. As one wise counselor put it, the New Testament tells us that "the Word became flesh," not that "the Word became a concept." [2] Though concepts are important, you are starting at the right place when you start with Jesus "in the flesh."

This truth can be confined within the message of no liturgical season. Throughout the year it gives authenticity to

---

[2] Helmut Thielicke, *Out of the Depths* (Grand Rapids: Wm. B. Eerdmans Publishing Co., 1962), pp. 76 ff.

the preached word, yet Christmastide commissions the preacher to herald it with keynote emphasis. The lectionaries highlight this doctrine—witness two epistles and two gospels which recur in the Christmastide lessons.[3]

John 1:1-18 offers threefold support for its declaration that "the Word became flesh and dwelt among us, full of grace and truth; we have beheld his glory, glory as of the only Son from the Father":

1. Though the powers of darkness struggle to overcome, the light proves unquenchable in him (vs. 5).

2. To those who believe in him, he gives power to become children of God (vs. 12).

3. From him we receive the blessings of continuing growth, "grace upon grace" (vs. 16).

Luke 2:1-14, telling the nativity story in all its beauty, centers in two movements that delineate the doctrine of the Incarnation:

1. He came as a child of earth born in humble humanity. "And she gave birth to her first-born son and wrapped him in swaddling cloths, and laid him in a manger, because there was no place for them in the inn" (vs. 7).

2. He came as Christ and Savior bringing God's heavenly gifts. "And the angel said to them, 'Be not afraid; for behold, I bring you good news of great joy which will come to all the people; for to you is born this day in the city of David a Savior, who is Christ the Lord" (vss. 10-11).

Gal. 4:1-7 celebrates the power of the Incarnation to transform the whole atmosphere in which we live:

[3] For lectionary sources, see p. 89.

1. Christ came as God's Son, to adopt us into a life filled with the wonder of belonging to God.

2. Christ came in full humanity—"born of woman, born under the law"—to save us from the futile struggle to make something of ourselves by following a code of rules.

Heb. 1:1-12 articulates in full detail the message that God, not merely *sending* Jesus or coming *with* him, was present and acting *in* him. Because this scripture sets forth what the church has sought to express in its great formulations of this doctrine, we turn now to explore the first four verses of this passage. If a single proposition can gather up its treasure, it may be summarized as saying: God spoke his final word, performed his central act in Jesus who is the Christ, to reconcile our estrangement and purify our sins.

When God Spoke His Ultimate

In Christ, God spoke not his first but his culminating word. He came as no stranger. "In many and various ways God spoke of old to our fathers by the prophets." (Heb. 1:1.)

Through Amos and Micah he issued a stern ethical demand:

> But let justice roll down like waters,
>   and righteousness like an ever-flowing stream.
> —Amos 5:24

Without this true and necessary word our thought of God would remain cheap and our life tawdry. Yet it called to a steep ascent of heaven too strenuous for our poor powers. Each of us learns, sooner or later, that the demands of righteousness based on any worthy code outrun our capacities for

113

virtue. Law, important and needed first word, required another for its completion: "The law was our custodian until Christ came, that we might be justified by faith" (Gal. 3:24).

Through Hosea God spoke the welcome word of love. Against the background of the poignant story of the prophet's love, buying back the unfaithful Gomer, renewing her life and dignity, came the announcement that God's own love is the source of all power to endure and redeem:

> Yet it was I who taught Ephraim to
>   walk,
> I took them up in my arms;
> but they did not know that I healed
>   them.
> I led them with cords of compassion,
>   with the bands of love.
>   —Hos. 11:3-4

Yet the story of suffering love in Hosea's household was not sufficient to point to the love of God. Another word was needed: "For God so loved the world that he gave his only Son, that whoever believes in him should not perish but have eternal life." (John 3:16.)

Through the prophet of the Exile, God spoke of the suffering servant:

> But he was wounded for our transgressions,
>   he was bruised for our iniquities;
> upon him was the chastisement that made
>   us whole,
>   and with his stripes we are healed.
>   —Isa. 53:5

Who could render this healing service? Israel as God's people? A remnant returned from Exile? Commanding the vision, heartbreaking the disappointment of its unfulfilled hope. The haunting, elusive lines sang themselves in the heart as a cry of unanswered need until Calvary made them a song of gratitude that Christ had "emptied himself, taking the form of a servant. . . . and [becoming] obedient unto death, even death on a cross" (Phil. 2:7-8).

In prophetic spirits of our time a needed ethical mandate calls to a struggle for order in a disarmed and law-abiding world. A distinguished philosopher describes our plight as, victorious in a war waged to achieve freedom from fear, we cower in ever-deepening terror. Under these ironic conditions, he asks, how can Jesus be the hope of the world? If we Christians temporize that Christ's "kingdom is not of this world"; if we evidence no urgent concern with the threat of nuclear annihilation—the philosopher continues—we need not be surprised that men regard our faith as an unfortunate hoax. Nature's deepest law, the law of self-preservation, he declares, now commands: "Cooperate or perish." Nationalism has become the sin against mankind; from it we can be freed only by according every man the dignity of a brother.[4] These astringent ethical warnings we desperately need.

Yet in themselves they remain incomplete. Is it true that self-preservation, speaking as nature's deepest law, can issue a saving summons? What if it should turn out that they are right who say that nature has another law, that of self-destruction? Can we be freed from the hazards of nationalism by looking on each man as our brother? What makes him brother? Apart from a still deeper faith about the nature of

[4] "Philosophy," Raughley, *op. cit.*, pp. 232-34.

creation itself, and of its Creator, what makes it certain that all men are my brothers—not my competitors or mortal enemies? The voice of idealism points us in the right direction, but we need that deeper word which God, through Christ, awakened in Paul: "The whole creation has been groaning in travail together until now; and not only the creation, but we ourselves, who have the first fruits of the Spirit, groan inwardly as we wait for adoption as sons" (Rom. 8:22-23). In Christ's assurance of our common sonship the call to live as brothers finds dependable support. Unless God speaks to us, we wander confused and lost.

Now God Has Shared Our Lot

This lesson from Hebrews declares that *God has spoken.* In Christ he has given his ultimate revelation of himself. "In these last days he has spoken to us by a Son, whom he appointed heir of all things." (Heb. 1:2.)

The question, "Who is Jesus?" is crucial, not because we need to find in him some mysterious quality called divinity but because we must know God's character. Is God like Christ? Karl Barth, absorbed in exalting the lordship of Christ, writes of him under the title, *The Humanity of God.* The church's long struggle to safeguard this doctrine against the tendency to teach that Christ only seems to be fully human reached a dramatic climax in debates in the World Council of Churches. In the first formulation of a basis of membership, the Council was opened to "Churches which confess Jesus Christ as God and Savior." So many Christians found that formula equivocal concerning our Lord's full humanity—so removing him from real contact with our life that we cannot be sure of God's real participation in our lot—

that the New Delhi Assembly revised the statement to read: "The World Council of Churches is a fellowship of Churches which confess the Lord Jesus Christ as God and Saviour according to the Scriptures and therefore seek to fulfil together their common calling to the glory of one God, Father, Son and Holy Spirit." [5] The added reference to the Scriptures— which characteristically speak of Christ as "Lord" or as "Son of God"—together with the Trinitarian formula, safeguards the real affirmation of both the divinity of Christ and "the humanity of God."

Christ is fully man, the gospel insists, yet in him God acted. The New Testament records never suppress his human qualities. His birth and childhood, his temptations, his hunger and thirst, his weariness, his sorrow and weeping, his suffering and death make that evident. Yet these documents assert unanimously that in him we witness God's act. Heb. 1:2 is typical in making God the subject of the verbs: God "has spoken"; God "appointed" him his heir. In one of his greatest passages extolling Christ's lordship, Paul pursues this pattern of verbs whose subject is not Christ in his own right, but God: "Therefore God has highly exalted him and bestowed on him the name which is above every name" (Phil. 2:9). As one of the earliest Christian hymns celebrates faith in Christ, the verbs are in the passive voice of which God is the active agent:

> He was manifested in the flesh,
> vindicated in the Spirit,
> seen by angels,

[5] *The New Delhi Report*, The Third Assembly of the World Council of Churches, 1961, ed. W. A. Visser 't Hooft (New York: Association Press, 1962), pp. 37 ff.

preached among the nations,
believed on in the world,
taken up in glory.
—I Tim. 3:16

Peter, proclaiming Christ at Pentecost, portrayed God as chief mover in his mighty acts: "A man attested to you by God with mighty works and wonders and signs which God did through him in your midst. . . . But God raised him up" (Acts 2:22, 24).

That God acted in Christ, the New Testament is everywhere clear and emphatic; concerning how God acted in him, it is less explicit. Although Matthew and Luke speak of virgin birth, the New Testament does not make this the key to faith in the Incarnation. Though Paul exalted his Lord through every symbol and argument his mind could conceive, he never appealed to special circumstances surrounding his birth. Mark, writing at an early period when his Gospel would be read with no supporting context of virgin birth stories, introduces his record as "the gospel of Jesus Christ, the Son of God" (1:1); yet he uses no birth story in support of this faith. John, who states his purpose in writing, "that you may believe that Jesus is the Christ, the Son of God, and that believing you may have life in his name" (20:31), makes no appeal to this theory.

Yet the mind requires symbols. Through the ages, Christians have sought symbols to declare the good news of the Incarnation. Employing one kind of symbolic language, creedal statements have declared that Jesus Christ is "of one substance with the Father." To our material-minded age this symbol has become less satisfactory, as substance has acquired

118

a connotation of material stuff. Originally it meant only that he was "completely one with the essential nature and being of God." [6] Turning from substance symbols, the Apostles' Creed used other symbolic terms: "conceived by the Holy Spirit, born of the Virgin Mary." Thus it denied the heresy that Christ only appeared to be human. He did not enter the world as a ghostly visitant, the Creed affirms, but was born, as men are born. Yet his coming was an act of God—"conceived by the Holy Spirit." In these vivid symbols the church strives to express a mystery beyond the reach of language.

God acted in Jesus, who shared our lot. In his humanity he moved amid uncertainties; he walked, as must we, by faith. In prayer he was dependent on the Father. "The Son," he said, "can do nothing of his own accord." (John 5:19.) Pressing the point, he said again, "I can do nothing on my own authority." (John 5:30.) My teaching is not mine, he said in effect, but his who sent me. (John 6:38.) In Gethsemane he struggled in an agony of choice among painful alternatives; and his decision was made, as ours must be, by faith that humbly obeyed God's will.[7] Standing with us in all things, he can be our Savior. As the Letter to the Hebrews reminds us: "We have not a high priest who is unable to sympathize with our weaknesses, but one who in every respect has been tempted as we are, yet without sinning." (4:15.)

He Holds Our World Together

From this truth the Letter to the Hebrews lifts up two all-important outcomes. The first is that God's Word in Christ holds our life together. "He reflects the glory of God and

[6] Bowie, op. cit., p. 60.
[7] Cf. Wahlstrom, op. cit., pp. 108-12.

bears the very stamp of his nature, upholding the universe by his word of power." (1:3.)

Not that the Carpenter of Nazareth built the cosmos! Whatever this may imply concerning the cosmic universe, it declares what every man of faith learns beyond peradventure: that Christ upholds our personal universe. Here each man's most persuasive word is autobiographical, resting not on argument but on confession. One recalls how, in extremities that must otherwise have ended in despair, the burden cast on him was lightened and carried to victory. We have turned to him in bereavement and found light in the dark valley, sought him in youthful quandaries over how a life's work could be made meaningful and found the way clarified by a sense of calling that came from him, kept tryst with him in days when doubts assailed us until in his company the eyes of faith were opened, come in broken penitence to him when we had strayed far in sin and found his forgiveness and cleansing new life, trusted him under crushing loads of responsibility and toil and found his promise of rest and the easing of our yoke no idle play on words, lifted our cry to him in lonely battles discovering his "Lo, I am with you always" not vainly spoken. In our confusion and defeat he so meets our needs that we can best describe our glad dependence with the old phrase: He upholds our universe by his word of power.

Just when any soul's universe is most threatened, he most saves. During World War II, hearing of a village where no pastor remained and all authority had disintegrated, where the women had been victimized by horrors that often followed invasion, one of Germany's great scholars went to give them protection and such reassurance as he could, gathering them in the church and school, where with their children they slept in the straw. Leading their evening prayers, he assured them that "He who bore our human shame from the very day of His birth was now among them, among those who had been shamed. If they were open to Him, they could experience His presence better than in hours of supreme spiritual loftiness." [8] So Christ, who shares the deepest humiliations by the power of God himself, restores our threatened universe. Writing to a girl who had fallen victim of these sufferings of war, the same distinguished scholar made appeal to this high doctrine of the Incarnation:

When these terrifying pictures arise, think of that other body that was shamed because He accepted solidarity with a guilt and with judgments in the midst of which He was as little in place as a pure virgin in a brothel. And if you cannot avoid the impression of the silence of God and your own helplessness and forsakenness in that hour, do not strain your will but think of the helpless forsakenness of that lonely figure on the cross who cried: "My God, my God, why hast thou forsaken me?" [9]

Far from speculation for quiet moments in an ivory tower, this great doctrine, most at home in life's darkest deeps, draws us to one who holds our world together.

God's word in Christ not only upholds our universe, it reconciles our estrangement. "When he had made purification for sins, he sat down at the right hand of the Majesty on high." (Heb. 1:3b.) With these words the thought moves from Bethlehem's manger and the Incarnation to Calvary and the Atonement; yet the two are observed aright only as

---

[8] Thielicke, *Out of the Depths*, p. 47.
[9] *Ibid.*, p. 50.

they are held together, as a triptych on an old continental altar reminds us. In its central panel varied scenes from the life of Jesus can be brought into view—including the idyllic picture of the nativity—yet only by moving a picture of the Crucifixion so hinged that no other scene can be reached except through it. Whoever preaches the good news of the Incarnation will do well to remember that altar. We hopelessly miss the depth, power, and high truth of this doctrine unless we remember whose birth we celebrate. We miss the Word God spoke uniquely in him unless we hear it as a Word from a Cross.

The doctrine of the Atonement has its own special place, to which Chap. 8 will give full attention. Meanwhile it is enough to see the completeness and sufficiency of what God does for us in Christ. "When he had made purification for sins, he sat down." Here is the answer to our wistful longing. "If only he could purify me," we say, as if, though he cleanses others, we ourselves have the peculiar distinction of being too great a problem. As if we even baffled God! To this John Wesley made the fitting answer in his comment on the line, "He sat down at the right hand of the Majesty on high." The priests, he noted, always *stood* to present the sacrifices at the altar. But when Christ had made purification for our sins, he *sat down!* The whole necessity was met; nothing remained to be covered; the entire matter was finished. In him God covers every need.

FOR FURTHER STUDY

1. Among the many excellent works on the Incarnation, two offer immediate help to the preacher: D. M. Baillie, *God Was in*

Christ (New York: Charles Scribner's Sons, 1948), and John Knox, *Jesus: Lord and Christ* (New York: Harper and Row, Publishers, 1958). A helpful sampling of sermons by contemporary preachers addressing aspects of this theme will be found in *Preaching the Nativity*, edited by Alton M. Motter (Philadelphia: Fortress Press, 1961).

2. For further analysis of sermons (see p. 50, exercise 2) this theme offers strong examples: "What Does the Divinity of Jesus Mean?" by Harry Emerson Fosdick, in *Riverside Sermons* (New York: Harper and Row, Publishers, 1958), pp. 265-74, and an excellent pair of sermons on the question, "Who Is This Jesus?" by James S. Stewart, in *The Strong Name*, pp. 69-89.

3. Noting how the Incarnation speaks to personal needs wherever they are most urgent, as the foregoing discussion has pointed out, lift up some personal or social problem now confronting your people and work out a sermon outline bringing the resources of this doctrine to bear on it.

❦

CHAPTER 7

Proclaiming Christ and His Kingdom

Ambassador or Paid Guest Speaker?

Any notion that the preacher is less than an ambassador of the kingdom of God reduces the pulpit from prophetic urgency to timid homilies on marginal matters. This diminished stature underlies an influential citizen's demand:

If their advocacy from their pulpits (in which they are, in the last analysis, the paid guest speakers) becomes sufficiently obnoxious to their listeners to cause a substantial decline in attendance and gross receipts . . . the clergyman mustn't be too surprised when the church fathers arrange for his transfer to more favorable climes.[1]

[1] As quoted by Franklin Hamlin Littell, *From State Church to Pluralism* (Chicago: Aldine Publishing Co., 1962), pp. 126-27.

If it be true that the preacher is a "paid guest speaker," this conclusion follows. How different is the case when preacher and congregation see the function as that of interpreting the sovereign reality of God's act which brings men under judgment or provides their one great hope. These alternatives constantly confront the preacher: to become a paid guest speaker or a teacher ordained to set man's life in the crucial perspective of the kingdom of God.

From the beginning, the call to preach has carried a mandate to herald the Kingdom: God has acted, a new age has dawned, obsolescence and death lurk in the ways of the old! The New Testament kerygma proclaimed our Lord's birth, death, resurrection, exaltation, and coming again as "inseparable parts of a single divine event." [2] The new age required repentance of those admitted to its life, who lived already in a supernatural world, on the threshold of greater fulfillments.

Though expectancy makes the air of the New Testament world electric with excitement, the resounding note of the first preachers is "that the unprecedented *has happened*: God *has* visited and redeemed His people." [3] Paul proclaims this marvel: "Therefore, if any one is in Christ, he is a new creation; the old has passed away, behold, the new has come." (II Cor. 5:17.) "He has delivered us from the dominion of darkness and transferred us to the kingdom of his beloved Son." (Col. 1:13.) We need not wait for a distant Kingdom; in God's decisive act it has begun. [4]

Wherever doctrine comes alive the pulpit rings with this

[2] Dodd, op. cit., p. 33.
[3] Ibid., p. 33. Italics added.
[4] Ibid., p. 34.

message. Despite the insistence sometimes heard, that the Apostles' Creed gives Kingdom preaching no root in doctrine, the Creed from beginning to end is a Kingdom document. God's decisive, sovereign acts vibrate in every line. He has acted in the coming of Jesus Christ, will act in his coming again to judge the living and the dead, does act through his Holy Spirit in the church for the continual renewal of life. Christian worship, habitually confessing this faith through the Creed, continually praying as our Lord has taught us, "Thy kingdom come," gives central allegiance to the doctrine of the Kingdom. We preach Christ defectively when we neglect the Kingdom—as if men could be saved in isolated unconcern for anything beyond their personal destinies. And we misrepresent the Kingdom when we slight personal renewal in Christ—as if all that mattered were a new order we men are called to "build." To proclaim the gospel is to preach Christ and his kingdom.

Focus of Jesus' Preaching

When Jesus preached, the Kingdom focused attention. Note how Mark tells the story. After his cursory introduction of John's ministry and our Lord's baptism and wilderness temptation, he opens the main story with the words: "Now after John was arrested, Jesus came into Galilee, preaching the gospel of God, and saying, 'The time is fulfilled, and the kingdom of God is at hand; repent, and believe in the gospel'" (Mark 1:14-15). Matthew prefaces his account of Jesus' ministry with a similar summary: "From that time Jesus began to preach, saying, 'Repent, for the kingdom of heaven is at hand" (Matt. 4:17). Plainly both evangelists thus announce

126

the principal topic to be developed in the message that follows.

Basileia, translated "kingdom," is no realm with boundaries, no new order such as a reestablished throne of David which the crowd anticipated as Jesus rode into Jerusalem. "Blessed be the kingdom of our father David that is coming!" (Mark 11:10), they shouted, unaware that a throne greater than David's was involved. The accusation, "King of the Jews," inscribed on the cross reflects the same misunderstanding

and shows that Pontius Pilate had him executed as one of the many Messianic pretenders to the crown, whom the Romans simply counted as rebels. Even the disciples on the Emmaus road say: "But we had hoped that he was the one to redeem Israel" [Luke 24:21; cf. also 19:11], and elsewhere the disciples ask: "Lord, will you at this time restore the kingdom to Israel?" [Acts 1:6]. But Jesus disappoints this expectation. Not once does he speak of the restoration of the kingdom of David in power and majesty, and of the Messiah who will destroy his enemies [Ps. of Sol. 17:21 ff, 30 ff]. Perhaps the obscure words "From the days of John the Baptist until now the kingdom of heaven has suffered violence and men of violence take it by force" [Matt. 11:12], involve a sharp, express refusal to have anything to do with the political Messianic movement of the Zealots.[5]

Not the throne of David nor the fulfillment of Zealot aspirations nor the reshaping of society in any way open to the idealisms of modern men was in the mind of Jesus. Nothing

[5] Günther Bornkamm, *Jesus of Nazareth* (New York: Harper and Row, Publishers, 1960). Used by permission. P. 66. The treatment of Jesus' king dom teaching offered here is indebted at many points to Professor Bornkamm's chapter on "The Dawn of the Kingdom of God."

short of God's sovereign rule in human affairs was at stake. In this he kept faith with the high tradition of the Psalms.

> The Lord has established his throne in
> the heavens,
> and his kingdom rules over all.
> —Ps. 103:19

> All thy works shall give thanks to thee,
> O Lord,
> and all thy saints shall bless thee!
> They shall speak of the glory of thy
> kingdom,
> and tell of thy power,
> to make known to the sons of men thy
> mighty deeds,
> and the glorious splendor of thy
> kingdom.
> Thy kingdom is an everlasting kingdom,
> and thy dominion endures through-
> out all generations.
> —Ps. 145:10-13

He held true to the deep insights of the prophets reflected by Isaiah of the Exile:

> How beautiful upon the mountains
> are the feet of him who brings good
> tidings,
> who publishes peace, who brings good
> tidings of good,
> who publishes salvation,
> who says to Zion, "Your God reigns."
> —Isa. 52:7

When the imprisoned John the Baptist sent emissaries to inquire if Jesus was the expected bringer of the Kingdom, our Lord appealed to the prophetic tradition as he answered: "Go and tell John what you hear and see: the blind receive their sight and the lame walk, lepers are cleansed and the deaf hear, and the dead are raised up, and the poor have the good news preached to them" (Matt. 11:4-5). The reference to Isaiah's promised day when God could come and save was unmistakable:

> Then the eyes of the blind shall be
>   opened,
>   and the ears of the deaf unstopped;
>   then shall the lame man leap like a
>   hart,
>   and the tongue of the dumb sing for
>   joy.
>   —Isa. 35:5-6a

Because these things are happening, said Jesus, "blessed is he who takes no offense at me" (Matt. 11:6).

The recurring note of good news to the poor which permeates Jesus' message underscores the fact that the new age comes as God's reign. He gives it to those who can bring to it nothing but their need. Matthew's collection of Kingdom teaching in the Sermon on the Mount begins with the beatitudes as characterizations of those to whom the Kingdom is given. "Blessed are the poor in spirit," it announces, "for theirs is the kingdom of heaven." (Matt. 5:3.)

The poor and they that mourn are those who have nothing to expect from the world, but who expect everything from God. They

129

look towards God, and also cast themselves upon God; in their lives and in their attitude they are beggars before God. What unites those addressed in the beatitudes and pronounced blessed, is this, that they are driven to the very end of the world and its possibilities: the poor, who do not fit in to the structure of the world and therefore are rejected by the world; the mourner, for whom the world holds no consolation; the humble, who no longer extract recognition from the world; the hungry and thirsty, who cannot live without the righteousness that God alone can promise and provide in this world. But also the merciful, who without asking about rights, open their hearts to another; the peacemakers, who overcome might and power by reconciliation; the righteous, who are not equal to the evil ways of the world; and finally, the persecuted, who with scorn and pains of death, are cast bodily out of the world.[6]

A long debate has raged about the issue whether this Kingdom is present reality or future hope. Apocalyptists have pointed to a promised Kingdom yet to come. Others, stressing "realized eschatology," have seen it as fully present. Still others read the Kingdom message as dealing with events of the near future which already cast their light before them. Without attempting to argue the matter, it is sufficient here to say that present and future are intertwined in Jesus' teaching. He steadfastly refused to establish a timetable. Asked when the kingdom of God would come, he replied: "The kingdom of God is not coming with signs to be observed; nor will they say, 'Lo, here it is!' or 'There!' for behold, the kingdom of God is in the midst of you" (Luke 17:20-21). He enjoined us to pray for the establishment of God's reign in our lives and in the world's affairs:

[6] *Ibid.*, p. 76.

130

Thy kingdom come,
Thy will be done,
On earth as it is in heaven.
—Matt. 6:10

Our part is to desire God's rule, and to live on the watch. "Of that day or that hour," he said, "no one knows, not even the angels in heaven, nor the Son, but only the Father. Take heed, watch; for you do not know when the time will come." (Mark 13:32-33.)

Parables Illuminate the Kingdom

In parables luminous for preaching, Jesus set forth the Kingdom in its double aspect as here, yet to be sought in faith and prayer. It is like buried treasure in a field "which a man found and covered up; then in his joy he goes and sells all that he has and buys that field" (Matt. 13:44). Already present, the Kingdom must be claimed at cost of all else. Like seed in hand, it holds promise of more to come (Matt. 13:31-32). Like a net gathering every kind of fish, it gathers all men; but as fish are sorted, men are judged by their fitness for the Kingdom which welcomes them (Matt. 13:47-49). Like the feast celebrating the marriage of a king's son, the Kingdom gathers waifs and wayfarers; yet the boor who refuses to wear the best he has is ejected (Matt. 22: 1-14), for though the present Kingdom receives him, he does not become a part of it. So Jesus played telling variations on one vital theme.

God's kingdom is not ours to build or win; ours only to receive in penitence and faith. "Fear not, little flock," Jesus said, "for it is your Father's good pleasure to give you the

131

kingdom" (Luke 12:32)—though the succeeding verses stress the costly preparations they must make who would live in it. Under Pilate's inquiry he declared that his followers were not Kingdom builders set to fight for him (John 18:36). In the mood of such passages, Karl Barth recalls the Japanese professor who believed he had found life's full secret in "Karl Barth for his inner man and Karl Marx for the external." With whimsical earnestness, Barth urged such men to "take flight from the two 'Karls.' " [7] Like his Lord, he would have us see that the Kingdom God seeks to give does not emerge from any combination of human devices.

No product of our idealism, the Kingdom holds us under judgment. Three parables comprising Matt. 25 depict our destinies as determined by readiness or unreadiness for the Kingdom. The crucial hour found five maidens unprepared (Matt. 25:1-13). They had resources only for the short run, sharing much in common with today's secularists, whose exaggerated estimate of the competence of science has persuaded them "that plumbing is more important than poetry, facts than understanding, the latest than the best, standardization than individuality, quantity output than originality, success than life." [8] God's decisive moments—opportunity, the birth of a child, bereavement, reverses—leave no time to prepare. Inner resources long laid by or long neglected tell the tale.

In the parable of the talents (Matt. 25:14-30), Jesus carried the matter further. The peculiar readiness that judges us is our stewardship of capacities entrusted to us. Two men,

[7] Barth, op. cit., p. 116.

[8] Henry P. Van Dusen, The Vindication of Liberal Theology (New York: Charles Scribner's Sons, 1963), p. 68.

putting their powers to productive use, were rewarded; one tragically failed. The nature of his failure is the point of the parable—as Jesus made plain by the dramatic detail and climactic highlights he lavished on this sorry figure. No merely careless laziness, his failure stemmed from twisted belief. "Master," he said, "I knew you to be a hard man, reaping where you did not sow, and gathering where you did not winnow; so I was afraid, and I went and hid your talent in the ground. Here you have what is yours" (vss. 24-25). Though others could take venturesome risks to succeed, his outlook crippled his daring. Offered the opportunity of the Kingdom, he was barred by his faithless fear—as are many men in every age.

In a third parable (Matt. 25:31-46), Jesus portrayed how human kindness to the least of our fellow mortals holds the key to judgment at the bar of the Kingdom. To be judged by our degree of compassion can be frightening. A secular journalist observes men's belief that "happiness comes . . . out of a factory chimney." [9] Was that why a senator scoffed that American Negroes need neither the right to vote nor protection for their human dignity, since they have more automobiles, bathtubs, and TV sets than most of the world's population? Too late, we learn that out of factory chimneys comes neither dignity nor compassion, lacking which, affluence can buy neither peace nor meaningful existence.

Judgment confronts us who possess the world's wealth. Infant mortality in southeastern Asia is four times that of the West, life expectancy less than half as long. Citing such facts about our more than adequate standard of living, a journalist

[9] James Morris, The Road to Huddersfield: A Journey to Five Continents (New York: Pantheon Books, 1963), p. 12.

without religious pretensions declares that is actually immoral "so long as there are still palsied beggars in the streets of Lima, or potbellied starving children in Indian railroad stations." [10] In a revolutionary world, daily events are judging this immorality. We Americans spend more every year for dog food than for the entire Protestant missionary enterprise, with all its hospitals and ministries of healing, its schools and colleges pushing back the horizons of the mind, its agricultural and technological mercies, and its preaching of the good news of God. Does this measure our compassion? In an insensitivity that undermines world witness lie the seeds of terrible judgment. This, the parable suggests, reflects the judgment of God.

Miracles as Kingdom Signs

Because the kingdom of God is most fully present in Jesus himself, preaching best approaches our Lord's reported miracles as signs of its coming. "If it is by the finger of God that I cast out demons," he said, "then the kingdom of God has come upon you." (Luke 11:20.) Others had said, "He casts out demons by Beelzebul, the prince of demons." (Luke 11:15.) Both interpretations were possible. The miracles are not offered as coercive proofs of the Kingdom nor of Christ's lordship but as signs of the nature and power of the new age that begins through him.

In the healing miracles God's reign burst upon us as conquest over demonic forces that lay waste our life. Present knowledge of the psychosomatic nature of much illness gives them a ring of credibility. We no longer speak of expelling

[10] *Ibid.*, p. 30.

demons; but hostility, anxiety, guilt, inner conflict, and alienation play much the same role. Against these, the healing power of faith and love which Jesus brought to bear on human ills still has therapeutic potency.

To those who confront the terrors of primitive life the demonic has no merely subjective connotation. A letter from a missionary at work in Sarawak makes its objectivity graphically clear:

It is hard for us to realize the terror in the night, the taboos of the day, the darkness of ignorance, and the despair of suffering and death that grips the hearts of primitive peoples—people who believe that all of life is controlled by evil and good spirits that inhabit almost anything and everything.[11]

Crippling hazards born of belief in demons cling to bird calls, the tilling of the rice fields, and customs surrounding new motherhood. A propitiatory feast to ward off the peril consumes a family's earnings for as much as two years. An old man whom the missionary had recently baptized raised an urgent, almost incredulous question: "Will it mean that I will not have to fear evil spirits?" Call these demons figments of the imagination though we may, their outcomes are tangibly objective and their exorcism by faith in Jesus Christ brings real and important effects. To such people the Kingdom comes as a new age brought near by the finger of God.

Even in the sophisticated West, we need deliverance from evil spirits if we are to live in health. Such spirits as materialism, greed, trust in power, and the war system lay waste our

[11] Letter from the Rev. Charles F. Root, Methodist Theological School, Queensway, Sibu, Sarawak, February, 1963. Used by permission.

135

life. The spirit of hatred poisons personal existence and plunges the dagger of violence into society. The spirit of racial superiority builds tensions in our common life to the explosion point. Is it naïve to see Christ driving out demons through a ministry like Martin Luther King's, exorcising the spirit of white exclusiveness and Black Muslim separatism, of both explosive violence and the paralysis of gradualism?

More difficult for modern minds to accept, the nature miracles of the Gospels speak of this same faith that God is present and active in the affairs of his world, ushering in a new age. Such a story is the report of Jesus walking on the sea as the disciples battled a storm (Matt. 14:22-33). Assured that it was he, not a ghost as they had supposed, Peter put the matter to the test: "Lord, if it is you, bid me come to you on the water" (vs. 28). Walking, fearing, sinking, and crying out for help, Peter was lifted by Jesus with the question, "O man of little faith, why did you doubt?" (vs. 31). When their Lord entered the boat, the wind ceased and the men said in awe, "Truly you are the Son of God" (vs. 33).

The preacher who hopes to communicate helpfully with modern men will approach such a story in frank recognition of their questions. Did Jesus come to the disciples by, not on, the stormy lake? May it be only a symbolic tale or a report of a dream? Has a pious legend developed from a simpler original incident? Does it read back into an earlier period some experience of the disciples after the Resurrection? Unless the preacher faces such questions openly, many hearers who most need his help will find it hard to take him seriously. They cannot believe he takes seriously either them or their concern about the truth of the material in hand.

To ignore these questions is to deepen the quandary of

thoughtful young people. Henry P. Van Dusen draws this summary of their resistance to such preaching:

The principal vice of Religion is its subtle intellectual dishonesty and practical self-deception; it mistakes probabilities for certainties, beautiful hopes for stern realities; it thinks that it has accomplished great results simply because it enjoys the emotional sense of great strength; it claims to be on the path to high achievement merely because it has made profession of lofty goals; it is sincere but pitifully self-deceived, earnest but rather futile.[12]

Left in this mood, they cannot hear the gospel. The preacher's final word on miracles must emerge from a dialogue realistic enough to lift his intellectual seriousness and honesty above question.

It is sometimes suggested that the difficulties concerning the nature of miracles arise from the fact that as yet we have no such analogies to them as to the healing miracles and exorcisms; but, since the love and power of the Creator and Governor of the universe were incarnate in Jesus, it is reasonable to suppose that "nature"—fully as much as human nature—would respond to him in a different way. The suggestion holds much of promise. Discoveries regarding the psychosomatic nature of much illness and the liberation which can come with faith, forgiveness, and emotional health have offered analogies which, within the lifetime of some of us, have made the healing miracles far more easily credible. Similar analogies may one day appear in other aspects of the natural world. Meanwhile, however, these stories remain diffi-

[12] Op. cit., p. 67.

137

cult to reconcile with other aspects of our experience. The issue is not whether God *could* act in such ways, but whether he *does* so act. Without prejudging this question, we have another avenue of interpretation open to us.

This story seems to have found its place in the gospel less for what it says about walking on water than for its word concerning the struggle of doubt with faith, and its final confession: "Truly you are the Son of God." It seeks to say that God acts as Jesus acted, cares as Jesus cared. His aid is never proven in advance; the man of faith, like Peter on the sea, finds the power of God only when he adventures in advance of proof.

Dietrich Bonhoeffer, who paid with his life for his witness in the face of Nazi paganism, paralleled Peter's response in a note he wrote from prison. "I believe God will give us all the power we need to resist in all time of distress," he wrote. "But he never gives it in advance, lest we should rely upon ourselves and not on him alone." [13] In either today's world or the storms of persecution in Peter's first-century Rome, the urgent need is not power to walk on water but faith to stand against fiery trials. In all such perils this story speaks powerfully of a Lord still extending a sustaining hand and asking the same question: "O man of little faith, why did you doubt?"

The man who answers, "Truly you are the Son of God," is declaring his conviction that in Jesus he sees no cosmic accident but a glimpse into reality itself. In Jesus he sees the nature of God. The universe, not impersonal and uncaring, is the creation of a loving Father whose character and relation

---

[13] Dietrich Bonhoeffer, *Letters and Papers from Prison* (Macmillan Paperbacks Edition; New York: The Macmillan Company, 1962), p. 27.

to his creatures Jesus fully reflects. In this faith we can best make sense of our experience, be most completely ourselves, live most harmoniously with others, and glimpse goals that make life worth living. Fearful of threatening storms, we find faith's renewal of courage. "There is much I do not understand about Peter on the waves of Galilee," runs the testimony of men who live by this faith, "but Christ has held me steady when storms of temptation and trouble were about to destroy me. Not because Peter walked on water but because when I was sinking in sin, loneliness, and fear he saved me, I say, 'Truly you are the Son of God.' "

Such an approach to the miracles through double analysis with the experience of the reign of God in our affairs can restore them to a vital place in modern preaching of the Kingdom.

Distilled from the Church's Experience

Although a message so vital can brook no confinement within calendar seasons, the church's long experience distilled in the Christian year gives it unquestioned right of way in Epiphany and Kingdomtide. The Epiphany gospel (Matt. 2:1-12), narrating the visit of wise men from afar to the infant Jesus, suggests that the revelation in him is for all peoples. Because the church through the centuries has seen this as a missionary theme, the world outreach of the gospel dominates the message that runs through Epiphanytide.

Historic lectionaries and modern church customs combine to make this season vibrant with the gospel's impact on human relations. Brotherhood Sunday invites attention to the truth that the more deeply a man loves his own Lord the more his eyes are opened to the right of others to practice

139

their faith unhampered by prejudice, and that the missionary approach to men of other faiths proceeds over bridges of mutual understanding and respect. Race Relations Sunday calls for practical probing of current meanings of the dignity Christ brings to every man. Closing the season, most lectionaries choose for the Sunday before Lent a lesson from I Cor. 13, with its affirmation of love as the key to all true relationships.

This theme of the gospel's outreach into all the life of all the world shares the keynote emphasis in Epiphanytide with the affirmation that in Christ God stands revealed. Peter's expression of the kerygma comes to the fore, with its proclamation that "God anointed Jesus of Nazareth with the Holy Spirit and with power; . . . he went about doing good and healing all that were oppressed by the devil, for God was with him" (Acts 10:38). Crucially important is this insistence on Christ's known character expressed in action. If God's kingdom matters to us, the kind of God who rules it is doubly vital; and the character of Jesus supplies the decisive clue.

Clarity on this point is essential in today's theological climate. Historical skepticism questions the possibility of dependable knowledge of the Jesus of history. Some interpreters make the existential encounter the sole criterion, leaving the abstract symbol "Christ" shorn of the historic characteristics of the earthly Jesus. The believer in such a Christ is left with no clear character by which to test the faith symbol. Too easily accommodated to our desires, such a Christ cannot save us from ourselves.

To first-century men, awaiting a Christ but rejecting the Jesus who came, our Lord made rejoinder:

Have you never read in the scriptures:
"The very stone which the builders rejected
has become the head of the corner . . ."?
—Matt. 21:42

In the parable of the vineyard (Matt. 21:33-41), he pictured a householder, seeking to collect his rental share of the produce, whose servants, and even his son, were slain by the tenants. The vineyard was the familiar Old Testament figure for Israel—and seems to have been so understood by the priests. For they "perceived he was speaking about them" (vs. 45). This rebuke of Israel's rejection of Jesus sounds a warning to the church as the new Israel—and to us who teach in the church—when we substitute Christ as theological symbol for a vivid and compelling Jesus.

Dostoevski's Grand Inquisitor was not irreligious in his outcry to Jesus: "Go, and come no more! Come not at all, never, never, never!" Finding his churchly Christ threatened by the ethical resistance of Jesus, he issued the ultimatum in the name of religion. When we allow the Christ of doctrine to lose touch with the Jesus of ethical reality, we too distort the gospel. Jesus is our norm. He is "the head of the corner." By him we align the wall.

At the climactic point in the Sermon on the Mount, Jesus exclaimed: "Not every one who says to me, 'Lord, Lord,' shall enter the kingdom of heaven, but he who does the will of my Father who is in heaven." (Matt. 7:21.) Thus sternly did he bind life in the Kingdom to deeds of ethical integrity. To dissolve that bond is to succumb to what Nels Ferré calls moralism in reverse, making failure the norm and supposing that continual confession can set it right. "This standard,"

141

he says, "is but another way of saying that we can be right with God by merely admitting that we are wrong, or perhaps that we can be right without any ultimates. All we have done, of course, is to make a god in our own worse image and called others to worship it." [14] These times call for preaching that faithfully remembers "how God anointed Jesus of Nazareth with the Holy Spirit and with power; how he went about doing good"; and, faithful to this bond between Christ and the Kingdom, avoids the trap of such inverse moralism.

Kingdomtide closes the Christian year with a preaching emphasis designed to strengthen this bond. The Festival of Christ the King celebrates the truth that to preach Christ is to preach his kingship and to preach the Kingdom is to begin with Christ. A typical lesson for the day (I Pet. 5:5-11), often approached piecemeal in sermons on one or another of the pithy verse texts that lie within it, challenges the preacher to deal with the wholeness of its resounding answer to the question: What sense can we make of the suffering brought about by seemingly victorious evil?

A sermon on the total passage can find in the closing words, "To him be dominion for ever and ever" (vs. 11), a thematic text around which to organize its thought. The preacher's double analysis of the historic background and our contemporary need leads him to focus on the proposition that: Faith's venture finds God's power adequate to our need. In the face of suffering and evil, no easy faith this! The text itself was hurled defiantly in the teeth of martyrdom. Paul had been executed; persecutions loomed on the horizon; Peter wrote that God's power is sufficient for every test—"To

[14] *Op. cit.*, p. 81.

142

him be dominion for ever and ever." It was no idle boast. Nero and his empire now long gone, what these suffering Christians built still endures. From this beginning the sermon develops three points suggested within the passage:

1. We learn the adequacy of God's power by humble obedience: "Humble yourselves therefore under the mighty hand of God, that in due time he may exalt you" (vs. 6).

2. We learn the adequacy of God's power by resistance to evil: "Your adversary the devil prowls around like a roaring lion, seeking someone to devour. Resist him, firm in your faith" (vs. 8-9).

3. We learn the adequacy of God's power by suffering in faith: "After you have suffered a little while, the God of all grace, who has called you to eternal glory in Christ, will himself restore, establish, and strengthen you" (vs. 10).

Having entered Kingdomtide with a Christ-centered scriptural message of such a nature, the preacher can go on to relate the doctrine of the Kingdom to daily work in his sermon for Labor Sunday, to educational interests that fill the air in the early fall, and to the expanding concerns that make the season vibrant with vigor and challenge.[15] Though no doctrine can be wedded to a season, the church's cumulative experience reflected in the Christian year guides the preacher in such ways as these to vital preaching of the Kingdom.

Specific Reform and Total Renewal

Through this doctrine, preaching best relates specific reforms to the total reconstruction of life. An issue in the New

[15] See p. 87.

Delhi Assembly of the World Council of Churches dramatized the problem. A committee report containing "An Appeal to All Governments and Peoples," which dealt specifically with issues of disarmament and world organization looking toward peace, was countered by a proposed substitute speaking less to specific issues and more to a general Christian witness for understanding and goodwill in such matters. After debate, the Council strongly approved the statement in its original form.[16] The ecumenical conscience became convinced that to speak effectively for the spiritual goals of the Kingdom in such a time as this is to speak with responsible realism about the attempt to apply the ideal to the tangled circumstances in which we stand. Persuasive, concrete preaching needs this note of immediacy.

Yet advocacy of reforms is not gospel preaching. To bring life within the Kingdom, under Christ's sway, is to seek its total renewal. O. Frederick Nolde, of the Commission of the Churches on International Affairs, important agency of the World Council of Churches, made this evident in a newspaper interview on a critical issue. "For what solution are you prepared to settle?" the reporter asked. "For none," Nolde answered. "The Christian community cannot settle for any answer. We shall press for the best possible compromise in the present situation, but we shall also press for a complete change of the situation itself." [17] Such are the practical implications of the Kingdom message. Living now in God's kingdom, we can accept no situation as ultimate; in the name of the Kingdom we are called to total change, beginning with any steps the practical circumstances can be pressed to permit.

[16] The New Delhi Report, op. cit., pp. 38 ff., 280-84.
[17] Cf. Niles, op. cit., p. 76.

In his novel, A Handful of Blackberries, Ignazio Silone symbolizes the struggle for reforms in their relation to the mightier force of the Kingdom. In this modern epic, fugitives, the unwashed, the dumb oppressed, the incorrigible resisters of orthodoxies are pitted against tyrannies which threaten to crush them. These little people stand between the extremes of an imposing array of dualities: two absolutes—the church and the Party, two robbers—the highwayman and the landed exploiter, two heretics—the Jewess and the renegade Catholic, two tyrannies—the Fascist police and the Party hierarchy. The Kingdom cannot be identified with any of these.

Yet a more than human struggle is suggested by the symbol of a mythical trumpet which "used to be sounded to call together the landless peasants whenever there was cause. And every time the gentry . . . would be filled with terror and bewilderment; it was their nightmare. On certain evenings . . . it seemed the Day of Judgment and the Last Trumpet." [18] Like the man whose outspoken conviction strengthens another to take a stand, the trumpet is pictured as the witness that wakens the courage of others. It will sound again, Massimiliano believes, "when we really can't stand things any longer. If there's something that's turning everyone's stomach, and yet everyone is keeping quiet because they're afraid. It's a way of calling out to each other, being together and giving each other courage." [19] So it has been since Elijah's lone witness gave new significance to seven thousand men who had not bowed the knee to Baal, but had uttered

[18] Ignazio Silone, A Handful of Blackberries, tr. by Darina Silone (New York: Harper and Bros., Inc., 1953). Used by permission. P. 58.
[19] Ibid., p. 137.

no word of allegiance to their God until one man spoke his faith.

The trumpet holds forth an eschatological hope that—though men's witness counts—the decisive force enters from beyond human resources. To a toast proposed, "To the future of Liberation," one character replies: "Future in what sense?" "Whenever it comes," is the answer. "Next year, or sixty or even two hundred years from now." [20] Even so, Christians live "on the watch," praying for God's presence "in the end of the day, in the end of our life, in the end of the world"—whenever, in his good time, he is ready.[21]

Of hope built on this faith that defies adversities, the trumpet is a symbol. One troubled soul asks whether there can be meaning in their lives, and Lazzaro reflects:

Haven't you ever thought that there's something guiding the movement of the ants underground and the flight of the birds from one continent to another? . . . It doesn't greatly matter whether you know it for certain. Even those that don't know it go the way they must. Did you know you were to come here? Yet you came. Maybe the ants don't know anything about anything. They have such small heads. But they go the way they must.[22]

The scene closes with the admission that, though some are trampled under the hooves of the horses, an overarching purpose gathers up all the losses, cares for them, makes them significant.

By this faith men dare against odds, believing in an in-

[20] Ibid., p. 308.
[21] John Doberstein (ed.), Minister's Prayer Book (Philadelphia: Fortress Press, 1959), p. 52.
[22] Silone, op. cit., p. 314.

vincible force—is it God's kingdom?—of which the trumpet proves to be a tangible symbol. In a scene of desperation, the shepherd Massimiliano shouts defiance to the chaotic crowd:

So you thought you could seize the trumpet? . . . Don't have any illusions, filthy parasites that you are, just because we're old and some day or the other we'll die. Worms reason that way. They think they'll have the last word. But there'll always be someone to dig up the trumpet. . . There'll always be someone that refuses to sell his soul for a handful of beans and a piece of cheese. . . And at the very end, when the worms think they've won, there'll come the angel. He'll take the trumpet from its hiding place and he'll sound it full blast and he'll wake even the dead.[23]

In these secular images a distinguished novelist suggests the Kingdom, full of judgment and hope; never identified with any earthly agent, yet using the witness of many; binding men in a fellowship of faith, yet never fully dependent on what they do; giving meaning to the struggles of men, yet moving by a timetable that transcends our human span, toward the fulfillment of its own high purposes.

The picture recalls Mark's portrayal of the ministry of Jesus. "Now after John was arrested, Jesus came into Galilee, preaching the gospel of God, and saying. 'The time is fulfilled, and the kingdom of God is at hand; repent, and believe the gospel.' " (Mark 1:14.) Alan Walker puts that in striking paraphrase in his book title, A New Mind for a New Age. Our new age of crisis has its parallel in the New Testament conception of the Kingdom. Then or now, the new age calls for a new mind—which is the almost literal meaning

[23] Ibid., p. 311.

of the Greek word translated "repent." In our idiom or that of the New Testament, it is the urgent word of a kingdom shown forth in Christ's character, dramatized in his miracles, made graphic in his parables, and the key to meaningful reform within a total renewal of our human scene—a word to give urgency, relevance, and power to contemporary preaching.

FOR FURTHER STUDY

1. Notable among works on this subject is John Bright's modern classic, *The Kingdom of God* (Apex ed.; Nashville: Abingdon Press, 1953). For added help concerning miracles, see Reginald H. Fuller, *Interpreting the Miracles* (Philadelphia: The Westminster Press, 1963). As this theme relates to the world mission of the church, one of the most thoughtful recent appraisals is D. T. Niles, *Upon the Earth* (New York: McGraw-Hill Book Company, Inc., 1962).

2. This would be a good time to make two distinct approaches to your planning for next year's preaching. Using the lectionary most appropriate for your congregation, work out a plan based on the lessons for either Epiphanytide or Kingdomtide, recording the sermon ideas evolved from double analysis of these passages in your notebook. For the other season prepare a sequence of sermons on the parables of Jesus. For this work the most authoritative guide is the recently revised edition of *The Parables of Jesus*, by Joachim Jeremias, translated by S. H. Hooke (New York: Charles Scribner's Sons, 1955). For a suggestive brief discussion of preaching approaches, see *Proclaiming the Parables*, by Martin H. Scharlemann (paper ed.; St. Louis: Concordia Publishing House, 1963). Examples of how two able preachers have treated this material will be found in *The Parables: Sermons on the Stories Jesus Told*, by Gerald Kennedy (New York: Harper and Row, Publishers, 1960) and

The Waiting Father, by Helmut Thielicke (New York: Harper and Row, Publishers, 1959).

3. For your more immediate preaching, a sermon presenting Christ and his kingdom in the light of one of the New Testament miracles would be worth attempting. For such a sermon on Matt. 14:22-33 there is a possible "starter" available in pp. 136-39. After your own study of this passage, work out an outline for such a sermon. Are you still using the worksheet (pp. 45-49) in your sermon preparation? For such a subject as this, that process is more than ever essential.

❧
Relating
Atonement to Present Need

Oriented on Reality's Map

To an aunt's inquiry as to whether he had made his peace with God Henry David Thoreau is said to have responded, "Why, Auntie, I didn't know that we had quarreled!" Though Thoreau may not have discovered it, news of the rift has reached the greater portion of his race. When the psychiatrist speaks of the ills born of hostility, it is not so much enmity with an individual that concerns him as a consuming quarrel with life itself. When the therapist says that alienation is the underlying neurosis of this age, he is talking of men cut off from any living connection with the real Ground of their being. Existentialists of the Sartrean school no longer quarrel with God, but their resolution of the conflict is achieved by asserting that "God is dead." Wherever a man stands up to preach, this lost peace haunts the congregation.

In every land and religion, men reflect this troubled awareness of a chasm of separation to be crossed in their dealings with God. Their houses of worship tell the story. The Hindu temple suggests a man moving within himself in quest of God; its successive courts are symbolic of a search probing inward through body, mind, and soul. The Muslim mosque resembles a man praying, its dome his head, its minarets his hands lifted in petition. The Buddhist dagoba corresponds to a man withdrawing from the world, crosslegged, head high, unmoving and unmoved. In Lidice, rebuilt as a shrine to the memory of war, modern museum techniques keep the Nazi fury perpetually vivid as the projection of a man hating. Across the Channel, Coventry was rebuilt with the outline of the nave of the old cathedral grass-planted as a forecourt of the new, its altar site marked by a pile of stones topped with a cross of spikes from the ruined roof, bearing the inscription, "Father, forgive." Dramatized in this memorial is the truth enshrined in the classic architectural form for a Christian church —a man stretched on a cross.[1]

Only so is the breach closed. At the heart of the kerygma rings the cry that Christ "died according to the Scriptures, to deliver us out of the present evil age." Dominant theme of Lent's climactic worship, this gospel note cannot be confined to any season. It holds the center firm in all vital evangelism. Memorable pulpit voices repeat the refrain that, wherever the preacher begins, he must make his way by the nearest route to Calvary. Whatever doctrine a teacher approaches, he must

[1] Cf. Niles, op. cit., pp. 100 ff., and Francis B. Sayre, Jr., in Littell, op. cit., pp. 59 ff.

orient his course on the globe of reality by its relation to one cross-topped hill.

Time's Peephole to the Eternal

Not until he has clearly seen and deeply felt the need to which this doctrine speaks, can any man preach effectively on the Atonement. If he listens sensitively, he can learn from many voices.

Some of these speak through secular culture. The cartoonist lets us eavesdrop on a toy department salesman who tells an interested mother: "This is an educational toy to prepare the child for the modern world. No matter how you put it together, it's wrong." [2] All through secular society the facts which support this sardonic jest confront the preacher. There is the stubborn drag of events. There is the "Why?" that haunts men's sorrows: Is it punishment? Is it fate? Was Hamlet right to say that in some cosmic sense "the time is out of joint"? Is it thus that Original Sin lays its blight upon us? Indulging our modern preference for the impersonal, we speak noncommittally of man's "predicament"; yet, as the root of the word betrays, a predicament is something predicated—so we cannot escape the question: Who predicates this "predicament" in which we are enmeshed?

Other compelling voices speak through the minister's pastoral care of his people. The brokenness and separation in which all men live run through the burdens they share with him. They reverberate in the idiom of their speech: "I don't understand myself." "I just can't face myself." "I was beside myself." "I can't seem to find myself." They stalk through

[2] Cf. Jim Crane in Eversole, op. cit., p. 217.

the troubled situations that confront him in a day's pastoral calling: marital discord, family bitterness, industrial resentments among his men in labor and management, racial prejudices and fears, and a motley host of snobberies. They speak in perplexities his people bring to him: souls at wits' end, who cannot pray; depressed spirits who can find no peace; patients whose burdened consciences complicate convalescence; impenetrable loneliness in the midst of busy family life; anxieties at breaking point; the cry, heard in surprising places, "God no doubt forgives others, but I cannot feel forgiven." Like footfalls of the Hound of Heaven, estrangement and alienation follow him in his pastoral round.

Little by little, he learns the catch at the heart beneath the smiling exteriors his people exhibit to the world. A man on vacation joins shipboard festivities through a sunlit day, though the calendar brings poignant private meanings—July 20, anniversary of the collapse of the attempt on Hitler's life. "The same day," he writes in his travel diary, "on which many of my friends were swept into the terrors of torture and death." [3] The pastor knows how like that is to the facades of bright faces that veil depths of torment, struggle, and the dark night of the soul.

He who would bring the Atonement to men as the life pulse of the Christian message must learn to live with his own heart laid bare to this separation and brokenness. Our Lord made atonement for sin in a sense more comprehensive than moral wrongdoing. Deep within him the preacher must come to know the bitter entail of disruption and woe en-

[3] Thielicke, Voyage to the Far East, p. 8.

twined in this embracing need for a Christ who "died according to the Scriptures, to deliver us out of the present evil age."

It is the preacher's business, forsaking all easy generalities, to speak with such specific realism of the forces that brought our Lord to Crucifixion, that men see themselves in the event, and say, as Arthur Miller believes they must about any successful play: "My God—that's me." [4] Such preaching returns repeatedly to the historic facts. Forces that swept on to the Crucifixion were set in motion on the day Jesus brought both healing and forgiveness to a paralytic and so outraged the piety of the orthodox. He was driven to the Cross because he befriended besmirched characters like Zacchaeus and women of the street, and in his friendship for them offended the morally correct. He was crucified because Pilate and the high priest temporized with political expediency. His suffering on the Cross was a product of the indifference and cruel fickleness of the populace he had taught and healed. His agony was deepened by the unfaithfulness of disciples who forsook him and fled. The gross vices of outcasts combined with the subtle sins of the respectable to crucify him. These wrongs so duplicate our own that in very truth "He himself bore our sins in his body on the tree" (I Pet. 2:24).

Three principal human factors converged in the Crucifixion —the Pharisees, men of religion; the Zealots, men of patriotism; and the Sadducees, men of urbanity and culture. Even good things, as men count virtue, conspired to crucify him. Engaged in a mission, not to win God's forgiveness but to bring it to us, he fell victim of the values we most cherish.

[4] As quoted by Earle W. Fike, Jr., in The Pulpit, March, 1963, p. 69.

No man has seen the Cross as saving until it has brought him the stabbing insight, "This is who I am, the betrayer who crucified Christ." Until he sees that, no man can see "the wonder of redeeming love," or learn to say, "This is who God is, who bore all this at my hands because he loved me—'O Love that wilt not let me go'!"

This double vision can knit the lonely and estranged into solidarity. The man who has learned to see himself as betrayer and crucifier sees his guilt in a new dimension, no less terrible in its wrong, but no longer his lone burden. He shares our universal guilt. But he is drawn into the deeper, saving solidarity of those who accept God's love and see in every man a brother for whom Christ died.

To the estranged the Cross shows a suffering, seeking God. The high Christology of Phil. 2:5-11 celebrates a divine Majesty: "Every tongue [shall] confess that Jesus Christ is Lord, to the glory of God the Father" (vs. 11). But this Majesty dwells in one who suffers, "who, though he was in the form of God, did not count equality with God a thing to be grasped, but emptied himself, taking the form of a servant, . . . and became obedient unto death, even death on a cross" (vss. 6-8). This Pauline anthem sings of Christ the servant in tones that echo another servant song:

> He was despised and rejected by men;
>> a man of sorrows, and acquainted with grief;
> and as one from whom men hide their faces
>> he was despised, and we esteemed him not.
>
> Surely he has borne our griefs
>> and carried our sorrows;

.　　.　　.　　.　　.　　.　　.　　.

> upon him was the chastisement that made us whole,
> and with his stripes we are healed.
>
> —Isa. 53:3-5

So long as this truth interprets the heart of reality, we need not live broken and estranged. To preach the Atonement is to help men feel and respond to this healing insight.

Christ's suffering search is the peephole in time through which we see God's search through ages and eternity. "It is as if there were a cross unseen, standing on its undiscovered hill, far back in the ages, out of which were sounding always, just the same deep voice of suffering love and patience, that was heard by mortal ears from the sacred hill of Calvary." [5] So say the messengers in faithful succession, running back to Paul with his word that "God was in Christ reconciling the world to himself" (II Cor. 5:19). Here we are at the heart of a gospel for a world off center.

New Testament Figures Address Our Need

By varied figures the New Testament wings this message to our need. John Knox sorts out five in his study of the Pauline letters:

1. Jesus paid a ransom on our behalf and thus secured our release from the slavery of sin.
2. He satisfied the requirements of the law for us; he paid a penalty we could not pay.
3. He offered an adequate sacrifice for sin, which we were not able to offer.

[5] Horace Bushnell, *The Vicarious Sacrifice*, p. 31, as quoted in *The Cross in the Old Testament*, by H. Wheeler Robinson (Philadelphia: The Westminster Press, 1955), p. 117.

4. He met and defeated sin and the powers of evil which had mastered us and which we had not strength to overcome.

5. He offered a perfect obedience and thus became the New Man, undoing the results of Adam's transgression and making possible our incorporation into a new and sinless humanity.[6]

Each of these figures makes peculiar contribution in relating atonement to present need. Struck out as sparks from the impact of God's act in Christ upon the needs to which the first preachers spoke, these varied images throw light on the human quandary as the preacher confronts it in each new time.

To men trapped by compulsive habits, it came as no light thing that "Jesus paid a ransom on our behalf and thus secured our release from the slavery of sin." The alcoholic must decide whether he can accept it as true, but if it is true it is unsurpassed good news. With vigor it underscores the confession of Alcoholics Anonymous: "We turned over the management of our affairs to a Higher Power." Not to the alcoholic only but to all who struggle with temptations that hold them in an evil grip, the gospel brings assurance that the victory has been won. This freedom, having come to countless other men who have accepted its reality and dared to enter into its new status, makes a credible offer to every victim enslaved by compulsive habit.

The second figure—that Jesus "satisfied the requirements of the law for us; he paid a penalty we could not pay"—speaks with assurance to those who say: "God may forgive me, but I can't forgive myself—I just can't believe forgiveness has come to me." In realistic tracing of the trail of sins—gross

[6] *Jesus Lord and Christ* (New York: Harper and Row, Publishers, 1958), pp. 174-75.

physical debaucheries and refined spiritual perversities—that brought Jesus to the cross, preaching can help men see that he bore consequences from all the kinds of sin there are. Yet for all the guilty ones he prayed, "Father, forgive." To them all he brought forgiveness. The message which has renewed men in every generation is no timid promise that God will save some select souls whose evil is not too deep. The gospel does not read: "God so feared the world that he gave the church in order that some might be saved out of the world." [7] The promise is inclusive: "God so loved the world . . . that whosoever . . ." As Luther discovered in this same darkness of self-searching which continually finds new sins to confess yet never feels forgiven, God's cleansing is not piecemeal, like a doctor treating smallpox scab by scab. What has been done for us is total and complete.

The third figure—Christ's offer of "an adequate sacrifice for sin, which we were not able to offer"—speaks to our sense of alienation. To the ancient worshiper who identified himself with the sacrifice he offered, its acceptance brought some assurance that he too was accepted. No longer did he stand alone, estranged from God. But in Christ, God himself has taken the initiative. He presents his gift to us as the pledge that we are not separated and alone. Jesus' acceptance of all kinds of people offers the telling clue to our acceptance, for he is the key to life's meaning. Identified with him, we are caught up into a great circle of belonging, the fellowship of the faithful, the bond of disciples with a Master, the family life of children with a Father whose love is shown in Jesus.

To those whose resolutions and prayers have been no match

[7] From a World Student Christian Federation pamphlet, "The Life and Mission of the Church."

for temptation, there is timely help in the fourth figure—a Christ who "met and defeated sin and the powers of evil which had mastered us and which we had not strength to overcome." In warfare with besetting sins, resolutions are treacherous allies. When a man says of some evil, "I will not do this thing," the statement itself projects the temptation anew into the forefront of his mind. His imagination and will conflict, and in such encounter it is a rare will that wins. Prayers that plead, "O God, help me not to do this thing," fall into the same trap. To pray thus is to enlist the prayer itself in pitting imagination against will. But when a man turns to the prayer which holds a victorious Christ before his mind in adoring worship, not praying for deliverance from the named sin but thanking God for open doors to new life, the whole spiritual atmosphere is changed.

In the fifth of these figures, the gospel speaks to the distinctive malaise of our time—the loss of meaning and the struggle with a world that appears "absurd"—of which Adam is the biblical symbol. Bounded by the nothingness of death, it sees our human enterprise coming to nothing in the end. In the words of Sartre's Aegistheus, "The dead have ceased to be—think what that implies in all its ruthlessness—yes, they are no more, and in their eternal keeping your crimes have no reprieve." [8] That is the inevitable conclusion, if there is no life beyond this one in which the dead can forgive, and no God to forgive in the name of the total moral and spiritual order.

One suggested hope is the escape Zeus commends to Elec-

[8] Jean-Paul Sartre, "The Flies," *No Exit and Three Other Plays*, tr. Stuart Gilbert (Vintage Books; New York: Random House, Inc., 1961), Act I, Scene II, p. 80. Used by permission of Alfred A. Knopf, Inc.

tra: "Why hesitate to disavow that crime? It was committed by someone else; one could hardly say even that you were his accomplice." [9] So says many a man: "It was committed by someone else." The man I was, I am not now. In the web of interlinking social forces and the tangle of hereditary and environmental influences, I cannot help being what I am. Forces outside me are responsible for what I am and do. The guilt falls back on the primal act of creation—as Zeus confesses in the play: "The first crime was mine; I committed it when I made man mortal. Once I had done that, what was left for you, poor human murders, to do? To kill your victims? But they already had the seed of death in them; all you could do was to hasten its fruition by a year or two." [10]

But these rationalizations cannot relieve the lingering sense of guilt. This reading of life's meaning underestimates that haunting persistence, which no trick of the mind can wave away. It mistakes disavowal of a crime for penitence. The verbal formula—"I am not now the same; it was done by someone else"—reading *backward* over the trail of personal evolution, cannot be substituted for genuine repentance which faces *forward* with a radically changed outlook. It misunderstands forgiveness as the erasing of consequences, unaware that to forgive is so to restore a broken relation that the consequences can be faced together and with a completely transformed meaning.

Sartre is too honest to rest content with the partial solutions his characters explore. As the play closes, Orestes emerges as something like a savior figure. "As for your sins and your remorse," he says, "your night-fears, and the crime Aegistheus

---

[9] *Ibid.*, Act III, p. 117.
[10] *Ibid.*, Act II, Scene II, pp. 101-2.

committed—all are mine, I take them all upon me. Fear your
dead no longer; they are my dead." [11] Assuming the responsibility, Orestes accepts with it the consequences. This imagery
borrowed from the Greek myth hints an answer which Christian experience finds abundantly fulfilled in Christ. Restored
meaning in an existence no longer "absurd" corroborates the
New Testament figure—"He offered a perfect obedience and
thus became the New Man, undoing the results of Adam's
transgression and making possible our incorporation into a new
and sinless humanity"—which speaks to the deep malaise of
our time.

Jesus took our bitter hatred into himself. All that drains
meaning from our life he bore, dying with forgiveness on his
lips, revealing love that awakens love in response. To the man
who stands outside with some doubting wistfulness—"If I had
your creed, I could live your life"—there is but one answer,
Pascal's word to such a challenger: "If you lived my life, you
would have my creed." In the end the Atonement is not
proven but accepted. To those who venture upon the reality to
which the many-sided New Testament message points, meaning and victory accrue.

Varied Theories, One Gospel

Deeply feeling the need inherent in our separation and
brokenness, presenting the message in the full amplitude of
the New Testament figures, the preacher presents, not
"theories of atonement" but the whole healing reality brought
to us in Christ. Freed from the necessity to defend one theory

[11] *Ibid.*, Act III, pp. 126-27.

or another as if it were the gospel, he is enabled to use all the theories, or any of them, as occasion may arise.

His message can ring with the assertion of the "moral influence theory," that the love shown for us by God in Christ liberates our answering love. Abundant psychological data affirms that we cannot love unless we have been loved. Only love begets love. Melted by Christ's self-giving on the cross, the New Testament asserts: "We love, because he first loved us" (I John 4:19). Captivated by this love, we are healed of the sickness of hostility. With healing comes power to live in quiet self-acceptance and personal integrity. The church, in which this love is accepted in joy and gratitude, is cleansed by worship which makes it "the fellowship of the daily unburdened." [12] Held fast by love seen in a Cross, it becomes a fellowship of crossbearers, as Paul said: "I complete what is lacking in Christ's afflictions for the sake of his body, that is, the church" (Col. 1:24).

The pulpit can sound the vibrant note of the "vicarious sacrifice theory," in which we are identified with the judged victim. As Sovereign of a moral universe, God forgives; but he does not cheaply disregard consequences. That the moral order exacts its toll, Paul reminds us: "Do not be deceived; God is not mocked, for whatever a man sows, that he will also reap" (Gal. 6:7). Sowing hatred, threats that breed fear, economic exclusions that impoverish other peoples, nationalism that plunges the world community into anarchy, we reap disaster. Sowing prejudice, racial discrimination, segregation the long denial of human rights, we reap upheavals that disrupt society. The innocent pay a heartbreaking portion of the

[12] Martin E. Marty, *The Hidden Discipline* (St. Louis: Concordia Publishing House, 1962), p. 63.

162

cost. Men discover the tragic price their misdeeds exact of their children. For men with insight to suffer, because of what they have thus inflicted on others, the experience sometimes brings awakening. At the apex of this moral reality stands Jesus. Seeing the cost to him, we see that God is no indulgent Father but the Lord of the moral universe, who takes our sin seriously, yet enters into it and shares the cost. To see this can bring renewal.

The preacher can make his appeal to the "ransom theory," which speaks of our Lord's victory over the whole kingdom of evil. This assertion, that Christ meets the total challenge, is needed in such a day as this. For men struggle against forces that seem to be entirely outside themselves, sometimes cosmic in their sweep. Some call it "fate," thinking of mass forces let loose at Hiroshima and Nagasaki, which seem now to have taken on life of their own and to carry their own inexorable threats. The onrush of automation seems, apart from anything individuals can do, destined to snatch from many workers jobs, livelihood, and meaning in existence. Blind suffering weaves its somber thread in and out through life's fabric. Some call it "the absurd." Some see it as a struggle with forces impersonally named—heredity, environment, necessity. In all this, with only slight changes of vocabulary, we are not unlike the men of the New Testament world, who saw that "our fight is not against human foes, but against cosmic powers, against the authorities and potentates of this dark world, against the superhuman forces of evil in the heavens" (Eph. 6:12, NEB).

In the face of all this, the gospel declares that Christ has won a total victory over the whole kingdom of evil. In his crucifixion, the personal sins of men and all the impersonal evils of the interlinking orders of church, secular culture, em-

163

pire, and militarism were hurled at him. Hatred, lies, the dishonoring of his name, together with the torture and death of his body, made their onslaughts. Isolated, he faced it alone. The crowds turned from him; in the Upper Room his band of twelve was reduced to eleven; at the gates of the garden of Gethsemane all but four were left behind; the four slept and left him in solitary vigil. On the cross his solitude became so deep that he cried out to God, "Why hast thou forsaken me?" No assault of evil was held back from this lone defender. All that it had, the kingdom of evil hurled against him.

But it could not prevail. Over this total onslaught his victory was complete. His final cry, "It is finished" (John 19:30), no gasping moan of defeat, made no crushed admission: "This is the end." As the Greek text makes clear, this cry lifted the shout of a victorious warrior. The assignment had been carried through to a champion's conclusion. Under all hazards, Christians have found it true that "this is the victory that overcomes the world, our faith" (I John 5:4). Validated through testing centuries, it confronts our brokenness and dislocation, calling us to enter the struggle with courage born of assurance that we serve and trust a Lord who has met and vanquished the whole kingdom of evil.

His words in the hours of suffering on the Cross serve as telling symbols of the reconciliation he brings to our many-sided estrangement. For brutal, treacherous enemies he offered the prayer of reconciliation: "Father, forgive them; for they know not what they do" (Luke 23:34). Into the circle of a family that had misunderstood and sought to restrain him as a madman, he spoke love's benediction: "Woman, behold your son!" and to the disciple whom he loved, "Behold your mother!" (John 19:26). Hearing the penitence of the dying thief, he brought reconciliation for deep guilt: "Today you will be with me in Paradise" (Luke 23:43). In agonizing pain, he made reconciling acceptance of the body's need in words that echo through all the fevered sickrooms of the world: "I thirst" (John 19:28). Confronting the mystery of God's seeming desertion, he spoke in no bitter third person about an absent God, but in faith's reconciled address to a God who still would hear: "My God, my God, why hast thou forsaken me?" (Matt. 27:46). From the heart of the ordeal about which he had lately prayed, "If it be possible, let this cup pass from me" (Matt. 26:39), he lifted the cry of reconciliation: "It is finished!" (John 19:30). In the total reconciliation of final trust, his last breath prayed: "Father, into thy hands I commit my spirit" (Luke 23:46).

So he brought healing to our brokenness. Urgency rests upon us to feel the hurt, to grasp the many-sided wholeness of the message, to bring it afresh to every lost and despairing man for whom Christ died.

FOR FURTHER STUDY

1. Two chapters on "Sin" and "Salvation" in William Hordern's The Case for a New Reformation Theology (Philadelphia: The Westminster Press, 1959) treat the Atonement not only with theological depth but with remarkable insight into the human situation as the pulpit must deal with it. James S. Stewart's chapters on "Proclaiming Forgiveness" and "Proclaiming the Cross," in A Faith to Proclaim (New York: Charles Scribner's Sons, 1953), are closely packed with relevance for preaching.

2. The foregoing discussion of the New Testament figures dealing with the Atonement could point the way for a helpful series of sermons, perhaps for next Lent. You will need to make

your own New Testament studies to uncover text material relevant to the respective figures. Such a project could take a worthy place in your planning notebook for next year's preaching.

3. Can you work out a sermon which brings the resources of the atonement message to bear on human needs as you find them sketched in pp. 152-54 and as you encounter them in your parish? Place the need on the one hand and one of the historic atonement theories on the other. Out of the dialogue distill a sermon theme, sharpen it with the worksheet process, and proceed to the outline.

❦
Entering
The Reality of Resurrection

Teaching Men to Die

The Archbishop of York has raised a question full of urgency for the church: "Is modern preaching teaching men to die?" Far from morbid, he says, this query is a plain way of asking whether our pulpits scan horizons narrower than those of the Bible's revelation.[1] Not preaching about death, but the avoidance of the subject, is morbid. Men know they must die, and the healthy-minded think honestly about the issue. When a preacher has straightforward Christian teaching to offer, he receives an eager welcome from the pew. All who interpret the gospel must take this question seriously.

Until we know how to die, we have not learned to live. In

[1] Donald Coggan, *Christian Priorities* (New York: Harper and Row, Publishers, 1963), p. 157.

167

his novel of "the lost generation," *The Sun Also Rises,* Ernest Hemingway depicts a circle of characters who, having shared war's brush with death but made no pact with its issue, live in a madness of escape. From their perpetual flight into drink, sex, and the wild adventures of the bull ring, they emerge as unsatiated and hagridden as they were at the beginning. Hemingway's own tragedy reveals that the story unfolds more of autobiography than its first readers could guess. After decades of artistic acclaim and adventurous bravado, violent death by his own hand came as the last bold challenge of an unfulfilled life to an enemy with whom he had concluded no terms of peace.

With an existentialist generation emerging from World War II, the matter is not different. To Camus life appears absurd because death levels all struggles. Modern man is Sisyphus, doomed to roll his stone up a toilsome slope only to have it slip back continually, just short of the summit. Matched against life which death robs of meaning, he can endure only by rebellious resistance. As a protagonist in *The Plague* is made to say, "All I maintain is that on this earth there are pestilences and there are victims, and it's up to us, so far as possible, not to join forces with the pestilences." [2] No escapist, Camus took death seriously, but only as the enemy whose sentence of nothingness brings the human enterprise to a full stop. With strange irony, his battle for meaning through rebellion ended prematurely in the impact of his sports car against a tree, confirming his friends in the feeling that struggling man is no match for the blind forces of violent negation.

[2] Albert Camus (Modern Library Edition; New York: Random House, Inc., 1948), p. 229.

This truth, that we know how to live only when we have
learned to die, did not wait for us moderns to unveil. Paul
took up the gauntlet death hurled to the first Christian generation. "If Christ has not been raised," he wrote, "your faith
is futile and you are still in your sins." (I Cor. 15:17.) We can
do more with death than defy it in our own strength. Boldly
Paul defied the skeptics who, like the hero of *The Plague*,
demand, "Mightn't it be better for God if we refuse to believe in him and struggle with all our might against death,
without raising our eyes toward heaven where He sits in
silence?" [3] Issue! counters a faith like Paul's. God is not silent
in a distant heaven. He has entered the arena with us, met
death at its worst, and conquered. Ours is no solitary struggle.
Death cannot write "Futility" across the map of life.

Here is a strategic redoubt in the Christian warfare. The
kerygma caps its recital of our Lord's mighty acts by asserting:
"He was buried. He rose on the third day according to the
Scriptures. He is exalted at the right hand of God, as Son of
God and Lord of quick and dead." Like a trumpet blast this
rings through the sermons of the apostles, lends authority to
the epistles, crowns the wonder of the gospels. Threading the
New Testament, it binds the documents into one potent
Resurrection witness. The shadow of the Cross lengthens
around the world, cast by a bright light from an open tomb.

Modern preaching confronts no question more pressing
than the reality of the Resurrection. To shrink our horizons to
narrower limits is to surrender a key stronghold of a centered
gospel.

[3] *Ibid.*, pp. 117-18.

Arguing a Theory or Meeting a Lord

Preaching that wins this case will stand, not on well-argued theory, but vitally shared experience. The apostles did not debate what had happened to a dead Messiah; they introduced men to a living Lord. Transformed persons bear witness that the meeting was authentic. Varied terms report their encounters. In Jerusalem on the first Easter evening, some recall, "They gave him a piece of broiled fish, and he took it and ate before them" (Luke 24:42-43). Others speak in terms less physical. The martyred Stephen exclaims, "Behold, I see the heavens opened, and the Son of man standing at the right hand of God." (Acts 7:56.) This is the language of spiritual experience, akin to Paul's terms as he presents his case to King Agrippa: "I was not disobedient to the heavenly vision" (Acts 26:19). Differ though they may in language, the reports reflect lives that point to one reality: The encounter attested its validity in changed persons.

The wise preacher learns that arguments about the empty tomb and the renewed body of Jesus are less convincing. For many a modern, such argumentation only deepens doubt. Resurrection doctrine is not contention about a tomb but invitation to meet our Lord. Resurrection accounts speak of physical manifestations not chiefly as proof that Jesus' body came forth from the grave but as testimony that the risen Christ the disciples met had a real identity with the Jesus they had known; the power of Christian salvation inheres in no mere encounter with a vague spiritual Christ. The key question remains: Who is the Christ thus encountered? Unanimous apostolic witness replied that Jesus, whom they *knew* intimately in Galilee, is Jesus whom they *know* in the power of his resurrection.

170

This priority of experience over argument directs the preacher. For though an argument can be answered by another argument, it takes more than argument to answer fact. And facts bristle in the Resurrection data. Preaching can take its stand on four:

First: Beginning with the immediate, there is the fact of the calendar. History's record breaks—B.C. from A.D.—at the point where a leader dies discredited on a Cross. Could a life on which such disgrace drew the final curtain produce this historic impact? Every week brings its reminder that devout men, reared to reverence the sabbath as supremely sacred, transferred their religious observance to Sunday because it was the day of their Lord's resurrection.

Second: There is the tangible fact of the existence of the New Testament, product of a burst of creative power so authentic that it has borne two millennia of sharp scrutiny, and grows more rewarding the longer one lives with it. Product of the pens of men whose secular backgrounds would support no expectation of such genius, it can be explained only by a profound event of substantial reality.

Third: Whatever men of today may think of the church, its existence, its impressive numbers, and its historic role in shaping the life of the modern world are facts. That a force so enduring, so world embracing should have sprung from "the march of eleven men," themselves obscure, followers of a Master who had died a felon's death, calls for accounting.

Fourth: There is the fact of the transformed disciples—on Friday night crushed, defeated, hopeless; three days later electric in their energies, indomitable in their hope; for an ensuing lifetime invincible under all obstacles, convincingly victorious

171

in brutally inflicted death, planting their gospel in one generation from end to end of the known world of their time.

Arguments can be met with arguments, but these facts speak persuasively for themselves.

Adolf Harnack's distinction between the Easter *message* and the Easter *faith* underscores the power inhering in an accent on Resurrection *experience*. The *message* concerns itself with the story of events which began in the garden of Joseph of Arimathea. The *faith* declares "that the crucified one gained a victory over death; that God is just and powerful; that he who is first born among many brethren still lives." [4] The message is important, its narrative a sturdy carrier of the faith; but it is the faith, not the message, that finally roots in living experience open to verification by men of this skeptical age, as truly as by any since the Christian gospel first rang forth.

Preaching best leads men into the reality of the Resurrection when it takes its stand on this core of experience, so long repeated by so many persons whose credibility is beyond dispute that it carries persuasive power to captivate by its contagion. Paul is such a witness. Careful examination of his life —as Luke recorded its exploits in the Acts of the Apostles and as Paul himself set down an unconscious autobiography in the copious open statements strewn through his letters— leaves little doubt that he found fulfillment of his prayer, "that I may know him and the power of his resurrection, and may share his suffering, becoming like him in his death, that if possible I may attain the resurrection from the dead" (Phil. 3:10-11). Paul's pivotal career is a Resurrection fact, stem-

[4] Thomas S. Kepler, *The Meaning and Mystery of the Resurrection* (New York: Association Press, 1963), p. 47.

ming from an encounter with the living Christ on the road
to Damascus—an encounter to which he never tired of allud-
ing as the permanently creative moment in his life. To it he
refers in his great discourse on the Resurrection, in which he
follows the account of the Easter appearances with his assertion: "Last of all, as to one untimely born, he appeared also
to me" (I Cor. 15:8). No passing enthusiasm erupted from
this encounter. It brought forth a lifetime of endurance, of
which Paul finally wrote:

. . . often near death. Five times I have received at the hands of
the Jews the forty lashes less one. Three times I have been beaten
with rods; once I was stoned. Three times I have been ship-
wrecked; a night and a day I have been adrift at sea; on frequent
journeys, in danger from rivers, danger from robbers, danger from
my own people, danger from Gentiles, danger in the city, danger
in the wilderness, danger at sea, danger from false brethren; in
toil and hardship, through many a sleepless night, in hunger and
thirst, often without food, in cold and exposure.

—II Cor. 11:23-27

When a man who has come over such a road writes from
prison, "I can do all things in him who strengthens me" (Phil.
4:13), his testimony cannot be lightly dismissed.

Experience of this order blazes a trail through the centuries.
No more credible personality than Albert Schweitzer graces
our grim age. Acclaimed by secular journalists for his great
humanity, he writes as a tough-minded historical skeptic. Despite much that was negative in *The Quest of the Historical
Jesus*, Schweitzer could not doubt the experience of the living Christ. Of it he wrote: "He comes to us as One unknown,
without a name, as of old, by the lake side, He came to those

who knew him not." [5] The creative, sacrificial life to which that encounter led speaks eloquently for itself.

Out of a career that struck out in new directions to bind non-Christian leaders to him in bonds of respect and affection, C. F. Andrews offered similar testimony. Of the Lord who changed his life, Andrews wrote:

> I do not merely picture him to myself as I see him in the gospel story, or only follow with vivid imagination his footsteps by the shores of Galilee. For I have known the secret of his presence, here and now, as a daily reality, at some times more intimately than at other times, but always the same Christ.[6]

John Masefield portrays Pilate's wife, anxious about the risen Jesus, "Let loose in the dark night, with no friend, alone." [7] No anxiety, now, could be more groundless. He is not alone!

> In every land a constant lamp
> Flames by His small and mighty camp.[8]

An innumerable company, the witnesses to his resurrection are too credible to be dismissed. More important than their words or their refusal to desert him are the achievements they attribute to his power and unfailing presence. With Joyce Kilmer, in "Citizen of the World," they say:

---

[5] (London: A & C Black), p. 401.
[6] *What I Owe to Christ* (Nashville: Abingdon Press, 1932), p. 84.
[7] As quoted from *The Trial of Jesus* (London: William Heinemann, Ltd.), Act III in Thompson, *op. cit.*, p. 82.
[8] From "Citizen of the World" by Joyce Kilmer, copyright 1914 by Aline Kilmer. From the book, *Trees and Other Poems*, by Joyce Kilmer. Reprinted by permission of Doubleday & Company, Inc.

Imprisoned for His love of me
He makes my spirit greatly free.

And through my lips that uttered sin
The King of Glory enters in.

When the preacher asks, How can I help modern men enter the reality of the Resurrection? the impact of a Christ who transforms persons yields a first principle: Do not argue a theory; introduce a living Lord.

Answering Futility and Despair

A second suggestion has peculiar force and aptness for this dispirited generation: Bring the Easter faith to bear at the point of men's sense of futility and despair. Disheartened individuals are not new to the human scene, but hopelessness that lays a cold hand on hosts of the most courageous sets our age apart. Ernie Pyle, one of the most loved men of his era, was no fainthearted weakling, as his war career bears witness. Yet Pyle spoke of "my wholly hopeless feeling about everything." "There is no sense to the struggle," he said, "but there is no choice but to struggle." In a sad summing up, he wrote, "It seemed to me that living is futile, and death the final indignity." The doctrine of the Resurrection points to an experience which meets the deep need of a generation all shot through with such bitterness.

As despair moves across the stage of our literature it often shows a strangely familiar face. William Faulkner draws it realistically in young Quentin Compson on his way to suicide. Recollected fragments of his father's philosophy float on the stream of the boy's consciousness. Through his mind echoes

the dirge that "nothing is even worth the changing of it." [9]
No recent invention that! Long ago, it took its place as
"sloth" among the seven deadly sins. For sloth, no mere laziness or mood of lassitude, bespoke a deep-seated inability to
act, born of despair that any act could issue in a good outcome. Nothing could sustain the effort its attempt would
cost.

To the mood of futility, ancient and modern, Paul ad-
dresses his Resurrection gospel: "If Christ has not been raised,
your faith is futile and you are still in your sins" (I Cor. 15:
17). His readers knew the very thought of such futility was
absurd. In the familiar martyrdom of Stephen, for instance,
they knew that futility did not speak the last word. Trusting
the resurrected Lord whom he saw in his dying vision, Stephen
had surrendered his life as no frustration. Paul's readers remembered the martyr's confident valedictory: "Lord Jesus,
receive my spirit" (Acts 7:59), and his magnanimous love:
"Lord, do not hold this sin against them" (Acts 7:60). Both
in victorious death and in present experience they had seen
such answers to futility that Paul could write, assured that
they would immediately understand, "If any one is in Christ,
he is a new creation" (II Cor. 5:17). Experience still makes
credible the apostle's triumphant reply to futility in the name
of the Resurrection: "Thanks be to God, who gives us the
victory through our Lord Jesus Christ" (I Cor. 15:57).

Responding thus to modern man's despair, the preacher
will need to make clear what he means.[10] Victory over sin,
death, and the devil are not readily apparent. Hearing this

---

[9] William Faulkner, The Sound and the Fury (The Faulkner Reader ed.;
New York: Random House, Inc., 1954), p. 61.
[10] Cf. Wahlstrom, op. cit., pp. 127 ff.

message, the man in the pew remembers two world wars, the murder of six million Jews, the long entail of exploitation and suppression that makes this an era of revolution in race relations, and his own costly struggles with grief, temptation, and the agony of guilt. Contradiction of the declared victory runs so deep in our yesterdays that, even in the first century, men were lamenting, "Ever since the fathers fell asleep, all things have continued as they were from the beginning of creation" (II Pet. 3:4).

God's victory comes—on "the third day." Persuasive Resurrection preaching must sound this note. From dawn to dark of Calvary's black Friday, the forces of good were no match for the forces of evil. When the sun went down, evil held the field. Jesus was dead and buried, his disciples dispersed, the hope of his kingdom collapsed, his reputation linked in dishonor with despised criminals. No angels had rescued him. No answer had come to his cry, "My God, my God, why hast thou forsaken me?" (Mark 15:34). Within the narrow span of any day, evil can triumph. Lies, violence, and treachery win the short-run victories. Evil men take shortcuts, while love and integrity go the costly long way around. Yet there is a third day; Jesus comes forth from the tomb. In the Easter event there is visible outcropping of one reality: Evil wins only passing victories. God does not crush it on the day of its triumph nor on a quick tomorrow, but on the third day truth and love—nailed to a cross and buried in a tomb—do rise again. In continuous warfare with the forces of darkness, faith has solid ground beneath its feet.

As marching orders in this warfare, the Sermon on the Mount speaks with power. Men who, eschewing Christian doctrine, say, as of a less rigorous faith, "My only creed is the

177

Sermon on the Mount," make it clear that they have not seriously read even the Sermon. They are in trouble from the first sentence onward, having no real intention to be "poor in spirit." As for bearing persecution for righteousness' sake, holding themselves to a stern law which roots out lascivious thoughts as well as lewd acts, turning the other cheek, giving their shirt to him who sues them for their coat, or trusting the Heavenly Father's providence for tomorrow—all this is ruled out by their disclaimer of demanding belief. More careful readers of the Sermon have regarded it as so difficult for the modern world that they have been more inclined to brand it interim ethics for the interval the first Christians thought remained until their Lord should come in judgment. Thomas S. Kepler speaks from scholarship and experience as he pronounces this sermon a battle plan of Christian warfare with a difficult world, undertaken in the power of a victorious Christ:

Had it not been for the resurrection of Jesus, the teachings within the Sermon on the Mount would have remained merely a collection of teachings . . . brought together by a Jewish teacher called Jesus, who suffered a martyr's death. Because of the resurrection of Jesus these teachings became the *magna carta* of Jesus *Christ* in the Church, the heart of the Christian covenant, the greatest set of ethical rules known by mankind, and a sermon which God's Holy Spirit will help mankind to employ, if individuals of Christian concern turn to him through faith for their support and guidance.[11]

A convincing modern demonstration of the final victory of God's forces of renewal over crushing powers of darkness is

---

[11] Kepler, *op. cit.*, p. 157.

given by the famous Vienna psychiatrist, Viktor E. Frankl. His fellow prisoners in a Nazi death camp believed that life there could have meaning only if they survived to return to the outside. He saw, however, that survival could be worthwhile only if life itself had meaning amid the horrors of the prison. In two realities no one could take from him, he found the keys—love and the sense of a claim he must meet. Though his wife was imprisoned in another camp, he kept vivid the reality of her love through long imaginary conversations. The claim upon him arose from a scientific manuscript representing years of research, which he had carried in his pocket when arrested, and which his captors had destroyed. Through all horrors he lived for his love of his wife and the rewriting of the manuscript, for which he continually made notes on odd bits of paper he contrived to salvage. Having found the way to victory over futility and despair, Dr. Frankl has since been able to help other men put broken lives together by the power of these two spiritual realities.

To the Christian this gripping answer to the blight of our age speaks of the even greater power of the love that bore the Cross, and the claim exerted by the Lord who suffered there. The Resurrection brings lasting assurance that through this love and its claim, God renews life "on the third day."

Confronting Death's Reality

One further suggestion presents itself to the preacher who would help men enter this reality: Bring the doctrine and the experience to which it points into bold confrontation with the stark reality of death. Paul led the way with his reminder that Christ's resurrection and our concern for our dead are wrapped in one bundle: "If the dead are not raised, then Christ has not been raised" (I Cor. 15:16).

During World War II, one preacher made a discovery about modern men. Concerned to help his people in their encounters with casualties, he announced a six-week series of Sunday evening sermons on aspects of Christian belief about death and the resources for meeting it. Approaching the series with apprehension that the subjects would be shunned as morbid, he was surprised to find that they evoked a more eager response than any other series in his long experience with evening worship in the heart of a major city. By the same token, the seven Sundays of Eastertide are not too long for celebrating the victory of the Resurrection, the living Christ, the answer to despair, and victory over death.

For death challenges every man. Evade or mask it how we will, all men know their mortality. Medical advances in our time have given grounds for doxologies, but despite all that medicine can do, the death rate is still 100 per cent. From a New England cemetery comes the epitaph of one Jonathan Kilborn, who died in 1785. Aptly it states the case of each of us:

> He was a man of invention great
> Above all that lived nigh
> But he could not invent to live
> When God called him to die.[12]

Nor can any man of our sophisticated age. The wise pastor grounds the spiritual guidance of his parish not in evasion and

[12] *Over Their Dead Bodies*, eds. Thomas C. Mann and Janet Greene (Brattleboro, Vt.: Stephen Greene Press, 1963).

the pretenses of false optimism, which give this subject embarrassed attention only when it forces entry, but in preaching which periodically confronts this reality boldly in the light of the Easter faith.

Much in the contemporary mood would prescribe mere acceptance of mortality with such stoic courage as we can muster. Long ago, Francis Bacon couched such counsel in the lean style of his essays. The claim runs

that there is no passion in the mind of man, so weak, but it mates, and masters, the fear of death. . . . Revenge triumphs over death; love slights it; honor aspireth to it; grief flieth to it; fear preoccupateth it; nay, we read, after Otho the emperor had slain himself, pity (which is the tenderest of affections) provoked many to die, out of mere compassion to their sovereign, and as the truest sort of followers.[13]

Yet even Bacon saw some limitations built into his conclusion that "therefore, death is no such terrible enemy." These mitigations of death, he confessed, could apply chiefly to the man who responds to its summons after he "hath obtained worthy ends, and expectations." [14] An exception so notable invalidates the counsel. For what is to be said to those whose lives are strewn with privation or blighted with failure? What to the millions doomed—by war, calamity, epidemic, and the massive poverty that engulfs the greater share of the human race—to premature and unfulfilled death?

How insecure are such defenses when death seizes one we dearly love! Despite her epic heroism, Marie Curie was vul-

[13] "Of Death," *The Essays* (Mount Vernon, N. Y.: Peter Pauper Press), p. 13.
[14] *Ibid.*, p. 14.

nerable at this point. Grief for the accidental death of her beloved Pierre left her in a hopeless abyss. Her diary entry on the evening of the funeral tells the crushing tale: "Pierre is sleeping his last sleep beneath the earth. It is the end of everything, everything, everything." Her biography presents a wild scene, weeks later, in which Madam Curie, disposing of Pierre's clothing, came upon the suit he had been wearing the day of the accident, bits of decomposing skin still clinging to it. Hysterically she clutched the garment, kissing the fragments of decay again and again, until her sister, who had been helping her, forced the material from her hands and threw it into the flames.[15]

Rich though her resources were in many other ways, Madam Curie's philosophy, which allowed no possibility that anything remained beyond Pierre's shattered body, left her exposed to the full crushing power of death as absolute and final. When faith opens no highways beyond a credo like Bertrand Russell's "When I die I shall rot, and nothing of my ego will survive," the stoic armor of "acceptance" offers thin defense.

How different is the case of those who build their approach to death on trust in him who said, "Because I live, you will live also" (John 14:19). Reason glimpses some intimations of the survival of personal identity beyond death. It sees miraculous feats accomplished as mind disciplines and controls a shattered body. It sees the miracle of memory maintaining personal identity with the self we have been, in spite of the body changes wrought by years and the completed cycles of cell replacement. It sees nature's conservation of en-

[15] John Sutherland Bonnell, *I Believe in Immortality* (Nashville: Abingdon Press, 1959), p. 48.

ergy and argues that personality, the highest energy, cannot be wasted. But in the end, all intimations borrow their force from faith that the world is presided over by the power and love of the God and Father of our Lord Jesus Christ. Short of this faith and its confidence in the Resurrection, the arguments, adrift from a major premise, have no force.

In a notable doctrinal sermon, James S. Stewart speaks of "Signposts to Immortality." Earthly rationalities take him only a little way on a journey which faith magnificently completes. The progression is clear in the "signposts" as he names them: (a) the fact of the reality of the unseen, (b) the rationality of the universe, (c) the character of God, (d) the Christian experience of regeneration; (e) the Resurrection of Christ himself.[16] The faith by which men and women stand up to life because they have learned to look death in the face, rests back at last on the foundation which supported Paul when he exclaimed: "Death is swallowed up in victory" (I Cor. 15:54). It is, Paul saw, a gift of God that makes possible such victory. "Thanks be to God," he exclaimed, "who gives us the victory through our Lord Jesus Christ" (vs. 57).

Does modern preaching teach men to die? To the degree that it falters in this commission, it deserts its post of duty in warfare men are losing for want of this message. A teaching ministry can help men to victory at this point where every man is challenged and where, in a secularist age, multitudes are defeated. In the power of this faith, inconsolable grief can be overcome: "Beauty for ashes, the oil of joy for mourning, the garment of praise for the spirit of heaviness" (Isa. 61:3, KJV). Such a ministry restores the expansive horizons of

[16] *Op. cit.*, pp. 229-38.

biblical faith, not arguing a concept but opening doors to encounter with a living Lord who restores meaning to bewildered lives.

In the closing moments of the brave sermon preached on the Sunday following his wife's tragic death, John Arthur Gossip recalled the scene from *Pilgrim's Progress* in which, from the swirling waters, Pilgrim's guide called back: "Be of good cheer, my brother; for I have touched the bottom, and it is sound." In bereavement's grip, Gossip said, he had found that true. So says the Resurrection in the face of all threats to meaning, purpose, and life itself: The Lord Christ, entering the dark waters before us, has touched bottom, and it is sound.

FOR FURTHER STUDY

1. For additional reading in the principles of this subject, see D. T. Niles, *Preaching the Gospel of the Resurrection* (Philadelphia: The Westminster Press, 1953); for examples of sermons by able preachers, *Preaching the Resurrection*, edited by Alton M. Motter (Philadelphia: Muhlenberg Press, 1959); for a systematic study of the basic New Testament material, Thomas S. Kepler, *The Meaning and Mystery of the Resurrection* (New York: Association Press, 1963).

2. Eastertide is one of the seasons that will best repay advance planning. The minister and congregation who approach this period with careful and sensitive awareness of its richness need not endure a "post-Easter slump" in church attendance and vitality. Begin now to work out a series of sermon ideas, attractively named, to be announced on Palm Sunday, beginning on Easter Day and running through the seven Sundays of Eastertide.

CHAPTER 10

Calling
To Repentance and New Life

Neither Without Our Act nor by It

Apostolic preaching arrived in the end where the modern pulpit tends to begin—at a call for repentance and a new life. The call—authorized by the good news—never usurped its place. "The kerygma always closes with an appeal for repentance, the offer of forgiveness and of the Holy Spirit, and the promise of 'salvation,' that is, of 'the life of the Age to Come,' to those who enter the elect community." [1] Remembering that, the thoughtful preacher may well ask two probing questions: Does my doctrine relate to new life with similar urgency? Or, reversing the apostolic priority, do I stress the demand above the good news?

[1] Dodd, op. cit., p. 23.

185

New Testament preachers reported a supreme event: God has acted in Christ. As the foregoing chapters have noted, they described his act as a five-pronged advance:

1. The time is fulfilled and the new age has begun.
2. In the birth of Jesus, God came among us incarnate in a Son.
3. In the life and ministry of Jesus, he revealed his character and began his kingdom.
4. In the death of Jesus on the cross, he won the decisive victory over the whole kingdom of evil.
5. In Jesus' resurrection and exaltation, he sealed his victory and founded the hope that he will come again to judge and to save.

In the light of this "theology of recital" of what God has done and continues to do, we see what our life means. Preaching loses power when it fails to give major attention to telling and interpreting this good news in terms which modern men can understand.

But a further word demands to be heard. *God's act in Christ is good news to those who repent by his power given through the Holy Spirit.* Peter concludes his Pentecost sermon in the classic pattern: "Repent, and be baptized every one of you in the name of Jesus Christ for the forgiveness of your sins; and you shall receive the gift of the Holy Spirit" (Acts 2:38). Like all good preaching, Peter's sermon was cast in the indicative mode. Not exhortation or lawgiving but report of good news, it told what is true. It made ringing affirmations about God's dealings with men, and the news issued in the inevitable demand—"Repent." Into the fabric of even this brief excursion into the imperative mode, Peter wove an indicative, the promise of the gift of the Holy Spirit. Preaching power resides not in whipping men's wills but in relevant reporting of some aspect of the vital truth that God's act in Christ is good news to those who repent.

Calling to repentance and new life, the New Testament preachers made it clear that men *can* respond, aided by the Holy Spirit. Ethical power surges when modern preaching recovers a vital grip on this apostolic doctrine. Repentance leads to new life, but not by our unaided act; God is present in it. We choose, yet not by our lone resources. In the power of the Holy Spirit new life opens onto ever-widening horizons swept by the panoramic vision unfolded in the third article of the Apostles' Creed—new life in the church, communion of the saints, forgiveness of sins, resurrection of the body, and life everlasting.

Neither without our act nor by our act alone do these changes occur. "God is at work in you, both to will and to work for his good pleasure" (Phil. 2:13), Paul writes. With a flash of incisive translation, the *New English Bible* links the imperative to its source of power in the indicative: "You must work out your own salvation in fear and trembling; for it is God who works in you, inspiring both the will and the deed, for his own chosen purpose." Christianity is more than a "Jesus religion." [2] It does more than remember Jesus or honor and imitate him. It deeply trusts him as the final power, exalted at the right hand of God the Father, resurrected and alive in the world, his work perpetuated among his people by the Holy Spirit.

Far from mere explanation of articles of belief, vital doctrinal preaching expresses the call to repentance and new life.

[2] Cf. Niles, op. cit., pp. 63 ff.

Every affirmation of the kerygma issues here. History's Lord may come decisively at any moment, therefore repent and live on the watch for his judgment and salvation. In Jesus Christ God has come to us, therefore repent and receive the new life he brings. In Christ his kingdom has begun, therefore repent and claim its gift. In Christ's death God has acted victoriously against all our estrangement, therefore repent and be reconciled. In the resurrection of Christ God has brought life and immortality to light, therefore repent and seek the things that are above. Redemption in Christ comes to completion in God's sanctifying gift of repentance and new life by the power of the Holy Spirit.

Through the Door of Repentance

Whoever enters the new life in Christ, then, comes in through the door of repentance. The preacher's problem of interpretation begins with today's language. In the biblical sense, "to repent" means far more than our current idiom implies. The dictionary tells little about biblical exegesis but much concerning the barriers to communication at this point. "To repent," runs the definition, means "to feel sorry or self-reproachful for what one has done or not done; be conscience-stricken or contrite." But the backward looking regret this usage implies shoulders out biblical meaning. A better beginning is the Greek *metanoein*, translated "repent." Its literal sense, "to change one's mind," emerges in Old Testament passages often free from any implication of sorrow for misdeeds. So even "the Lord repented that he had made Saul king over Israel." (I Sam. 15:35.) Whatever more the New Testament may mean by repentance, its significance begins with a mind wholly changed, a direction reversed, an outlook reoriented.

New life, a gift of grace, is not cheap—as if there could be forgiveness without repentance. Salvation is the other face of judgment; our "over-graced" religion needs to hear again the biblical warnings against the separation of these two realities which belong organically together. Jeremiah warned:

> They have healed the wound of my
>   people lightly,
> saying, "Peace, peace,"
> when there is no peace.
>   —Jer. 6:14; 8:11

An era deeply influenced by the "peace of mind" cult is ripe for that warning. In our day, as in Jeremiah's, preachers are tempted to soften the seriousness of the call to repent; but grace does not cancel judgment. As Jeremiah knew, "It is a lie which they are prophesying to you, with the result that you will be removed far from your land, and I will drive you out, and you will perish." (Jer. 27:10.)

When the pulpit forgets to be prophetic, the warning voice comes from other quarters. Even the light verse of Ogden Nash flashes its glints of prophecy in a whimsical reflection on global life or death:

> Now at the daily boast of "My retaliation can lick your
>   retaliation" I am with apprehension stricken,
> As one who watches two adolescent hot-rodders careening
>   headlong toward each other, each determined to die
>   rather than chicken.
> Once again there is someone we don't see eye to eye with,
>   and maybe I couldn't be dafter,

189

> But I keep wondering if this time we couldn't settle our
> differences before a war instead of after.[3]

Within the religious community, David Head speaks in
similar vein as he pictures Noah meditating on the flood of his
time and the dreaded fire of ours. No boat, Noah ponders,
will help us now! Would a bridge be a possibility? But to
help, the bridge must have piers very deep indeed—as deep
as an eternal covenant. "Thy covenant with man alone makes
possible man's covenant with man," he reflects. "Is the bow
set even in the cursed cloud?" [4]

Thus the biblical dimensions of repentance come in view.
Change of mind on our human level, it is more than natural.
In the Christian vocabulary, repentance is all but meaningless
until we see it in terms of our relation to God; just as sin
is misunderstood when we suppose it is moral lapse short of
the major estrangement our broken relation to God involves.
Repentance diminished to "feeling sorry" is part and parcel
of a view of sin eroded to "misdemeanor." D. T. Niles recalls
that his native Tamil tongue makes sin anything that reduces
man to a pitiable state. The Bible, he adds, sees sin as all that
reduces God to a pitiable state.[5] Sin plunges God into the
horror of Calvary, and repentance so reverses our man-cen-
tered frame of mind that we can no longer bear to hurt God.

In biblical doctrine, repentance is a gift of God. Men repent by the power of the Holy Spirit, who brings home to us
what Jesus taught. "The Counselor, the Holy Spirit, whom

[3] "Is There an Oculist in the House?" from *Everyone but Thee and Me.*
Copyright © 1962, by Ogden Nash. Used by permission.
[4] Head, *op. cit.,* p. 52.
[5] *Op. cit.,* pp. 54-55.

the Father will send in my name," said Jesus, "he will teach you all things, and bring to your remembrance all that I have said to you." (John 14:26.) Insight into the meaning of Jesus is so essentially the mark of the Holy Spirit that one theologian judges the validity of a religious experience on this ground. Whether it is the gift of the Spirit, he says, depends on whether it is "bound to the revelation of God in Christ." [6]

But dependence on the Spirit runs deeper. In the will by which the penitent turns to God he is a beneficiary of the divine gift. According to the early church, it was God who "granted repentance unto life" (Acts 11:18). "Do you not know," asked Paul, "that God's kindness is meant to lead you to repentance?" (Rom. 2:4.) Counseling Timothy to correct his opponents with kindness, he observed that "God may perhaps grant that they will repent and come to know the truth" (II Tim. 2:25).

This dependence of the corrupted human will upon God for the capacity to repent was spelled out in detail in the sixth century by the Council of Orange:

If anyone says that God has mercy upon us when, apart from his grace, we believe, will, desire, strive, labor, pray, watch, study, seek, ask, or knock, but does not confess that it is by the infusion and inspiration of the Holy Spirit within us that we have the faith, the will, or the strength to do all these things as we ought; or if anyone makes the assistance of grace depend on the humility or obedience of man and does not agree that it is a gift of grace itself that we are obedient and humble, he contradicts the Apostle who

[6] Hugh A. McLeod, in *The World Methodist Conference Speaks to the World*, ed. T. Otto Nall (Nashville: Methodist Evangelistic Materials, 1961), p. 72.

says, "What hast thou that thou hast not received?" (I Cor. 4:7), and, "By the grace of God, I am what I am" (I Cor. 15:10).[7]

As the Council went on to insist, even faith in God rests, not on our initiative, but on his.[8] It is reassuring for struggling men to remember that the same God who made the saints of other times and the Schweitzers and Kagawas of today is at work in us.

Donald Coggan sees saint-making portrayed in the west window of Chester Cathedral. From three interlinking circles which symbolize the Trinity fly the doves that suggest the sevenfold gifts of the Spirit—all the power of God available to make us into persons through whom his light shines! Yet— we can block that power! [9] Awareness of that truth haunts the New Testament preachers. Paul, calling the Corinthians to glorify God by obedience, makes it clear that obedience itself comes by the grace of God. So he concludes with the exclamation, "Thanks be to God for his inexpressible gift!"

One of the most representative statements of the Christian consensus in modern times, the report of the Edinburgh Conference on Faith and Order (1937), reaffirming our indebtedness to God's act in our repentance, continued: "But, on the other hand, it is the will of God that His grace should be actively appropriated by man's own will and that for such decision man should remain responsible." [10] Neither by our

---

[7] Denzinger, *Enchiridian Symbolorum,* as quoted in *Creeds of the Churches,* ed. John H. Leith (Anchor Books; Garden City: Doubleday & Company, Inc., 1963), p. 39.

[8] *Ibid.,* pp. 44 ff.

[9] Cf. Coggan, *op. cit.,* p. 47.

[10] *The Second World Conference on Faith and Order,* ed. Leonard Hodgson (New York: The Macmillan Company, 1938), p. 225.

act alone nor without our act does repentance open the gates of new life.

Into Full Maturity

Entered by repentance in the power of the Holy Spirit, the new life is a call to *endless growth* by his power. The cross on Calvary becomes personally saving when it is erected in one's own life, as Jesus said: "If any man would come after me, let him deny himself and take up his cross and follow me. For whoever would save his life will lose it; and whoever loses his life for my sake and the gospel's will save it" (Mark 8:34-35). Planted in us, the Cross saves by challenging our personal ambitions in continuous and progressive confrontation.

Freely received through faith, we are taken into a community on pilgrimage. Through Paul's pastoral care of his churches runs his constant concern for the continued growth of his converts. Note the "more and more" in his words to the Thessalonians. "We beseech and exhort you in the Lord Jesus, that as you learned from us how you ought to live and to please God, just as you are doing, you do so more and more." (I Thess. 4:1.) Or hear his call to "increase" in Christian love. "May the Lord make you increase and abound in love to one another and to all men." (I Thess. 3:12.) In the warfare with evil, half victories are not enough, he says, so he calls the Church to arm itself for warfare against *all* the hosts of evil (Eph. 6:10 ff.).

Many necessities urge the pulpit to renew its call to the unending growth essential to the Christian life. Secularism underscores the necessity by its drive toward conformity in a mass society. Popular religion requires this antidote to its easy formulas for a placid, successful life governed by stand-

ards drawn from the world around us. Some supposed orthodoxies demand this answer to the moral soporific of grace
preached as if men had no choice but to continue con-
sciously wrong, assured that confession of wrong will make
them right.

The Wesleyan doctrine of Christian perfection has been
derided as futile "perfectionism." The principle, "Find the
referent," may well send the preacher to check the source of
the doctrine in John Wesley himself. It may clarify the matter
to find Wesley presenting the carefully delimited claim that

Christian perfection . . . does not imply . . . an exemption either
from ignorance, or mistake, or infirmities, or temptations. . . .
Neither in this respect is there any absolute perfection on earth.
There is no perfection of degrees, as it is termed; none which does
not admit of continual increase. So that how much soever any
man has attained, or in how high degree soever he is perfect, he
hath still to "grow in grace," and daily to advance in the knowledge and love of God his Saviour.[11]

Who can deny the need for this perpetual growth? Where on
his pilgrimage is the Christian to stop, saying, "Now I am
good enough?" If a man is content with half-measures, can
he be said to possess genuine character at all? If he supposes
it is enough to be honest some of the time, when can his
honesty be trusted? Working faithfully some days, carelessly
on others, is his craftsmanship dependable? Satisfied with
half-truths, is he truthful? Is it, then, absurd to teach that
a Christian cannot be content with a life in which his love is

---

[11] John Wesley, Sermon XL, "Christian Perfection," The Works of John
Wesley (Grand Rapids, Michigan: Zondervan Publishing House), VI, 5-6.

limited and intermittent? Is there not sound basis for the Wesleyan quest to "be perfected in love in this life"? [12]

Preparing to preach on this theme, the minister may well trace it in the New Testament use of the Greek *teleion*. Generally translated "perfect" in the King James Version, "mature" in the Revised Standard, its meanings suggest what is complete, mature, perfect. In Heb. 5:14, it gives the phrase, "solid food is for the *mature*," and in I Cor. 14:20, "do not be children in your thinking; be babes in evil, but in thinking be *mature*."

If "maturity" fits the contemporary idiom better than "perfection," the New Testament call to growth remains unchanged, as a comparison of the King James and Revised Standard versions quickly shows. Note, "Until we all attain to the unity of the faith and of the knowledge of the Son of God, to *mature* [KJV: *perfect*] manhood, to the measure of the stature of the fullness of Christ." (Eph. 4:13.) Or, "Let those who are *mature* [KJV: *perfect*] be thus minded." (Phil. 3:15.) Or again, "That we may present every man *mature* [KJV: *perfect*] in Christ." (Col. 1:28.) Through the New Testament runs a thread of expectation that men will not rest anywhere along the way of Christian growth. Led to the kind of life they see in their Lord, they can settle for nothing less. Whether the idiom of a period calls that perfection or maturity, the fact remains unchanged.

The minister preparing to present this subject to his people will meditate on how long and earnestly the best of men have given themselves to the demanding trials out of which maturity has come. Tirelessly God draws such men to their full

[12] Cf. Nall, *op. cit.*, a paper by Gerald Ensley on "The Methodist Doctrine of Perfection," pp. 103-7.

stature. In its recollection of "Moses, when he was grown up" (Heb. 11:24), the New Testament suggests a heroic saga of growth—forty years amid the sophistication and learning of Pharaoh's court; forty years in the desert with its hardships, its lore, its long meditations; then the great years in which God used him to free a people. God opens the way to maturity through experience, testing, and the leading of the Holy Spirit. "That we may present every man mature in Christ": what ample dimensions that phrase, "in Christ," adds to the concept of maturity!

Like growth in the natural world, new life in Christ unfolds in response to power from beyond us. When repentance reorients a personality, a new life begins in response to Christ's stimulus. Thenceforward the Christian is called to grow under the nurturing of God's love and the Spirit's presence. From conversion onward he develops, "as one restored from death to life might be expected to be capable of progress from sickness into health within the life to which he has returned." [13] The New Testament word for this gift of growth is "sanctification," of which the Christian consensus in the Edinburgh Conference report offers a suggestive definition:

Sanctification is the work of God, whereby through the Holy Spirit He continually renews us and the whole Church, delivering us from the power of sin, giving us increase in holiness, and transforming us into the likeness of His Son through participation in His death and in His risen life. This renewal, inspiring us to continual spiritual activity and conflict with evil, remains throughout the gift of God.[14]

[13] A *Theological Word Book of the Bible*, ed. Alan Richardson (New York: The Macmillan Company, 1957), p. 218.
[14] Hodgson, *op. cit.*, p. 225.

Our growth, and all that we make of life, is only giving back to God what he has given to us. As a young man, Stephen F. Bayne, Jr., watched the acolytes bring the offering of bread and wine to the priest to be consecrated, and saw the priest present at the altar these elements which had come from God in the first place and were now given back to him by a worshiping congregation. It spoke to him of the call to present his body "a living sacrifice, holy and acceptable to God." "Suddenly my life began to make sense," Bayne says. "It had come from God; it was my part to offer it to Him, as our Lord had offered His whole life to the Father." [15] Vital preaching on this high doctrine can bring men of this age, stifled under a pall of meaninglessness, to such luminous moments of discovery.

Incorporated into Serving Unity

Entered by repentance in the power of the Holy Spirit, called to endless growth by the same power, the new life in Christ *incorporates us into the serving unity of the church* by the communion of the Holy Spirit. The penitent are drawn from isolation and separateness into the people of God. From his earliest dealings with Israel, God—not content to win lonely individuals—consolidated a people. "Now therefore," he said through Moses, "if you will obey my voice and keep my covenant, you shall be my own possession among all peoples; for all the earth is mine, and you shall be to me a kingdom of priests and a holy nation." (Exod. 19:5-6.) When his mighty act in Christ had brought the new age, he spoke in similar terms to the church as the new Israel. "But you are

[15] *Mindful of the Love* (New York: Oxford University Press, 1962), p. 63.

197

a chosen race," so ran the apostolic message, "a royal priest-hood, a holy nation, God's own people, that you may declare the wonderful deeds of him who called you out of darkness into his marvelous light. Once you were no people but now you are God's people." (I Pet. 2:9-10.) Thus his Spirit works to unify a people set apart for his service.

Apart from this unity in service, Christian witness loses its validity. A notable evangelist declared that a church can be used in evangelism only when it is dedicated to service to men at the point of their need, in the community where God has placed it. Launching an evangelistic crusade when it has failed to render needed human service, a church will not win men to Christ; it will distort their understanding of the gospel.[16] What happens when a congregation participates in racial exclusions while it invites men to come to Christ and be saved? Those who respond are brought into relation to a Christ diminished and misrepresented by attitudes at odds with the Jesus of the Gospels. The wider community mean-while is confirmed in antipathy toward a gospel which, meant to make men one, has been twisted to sanction inhumanity and division.

Preaching, through which men find themselves in relation to the Spirit who draws them into serving unity, can be transforming to men and communities. Such preaching led to the renewal of the church in Holland. The leaders of the movement said to the congregations: "You have to become what you are and, because you do not know what you are, you do not become anything." Steadily they presented for consideration and study a vital doctrine of the church. Little

[16] Niles, op. cit., p. 176.

by little, as men began to catch the picture of what it is really to be a church in relation to Christ, they would say: "Now I understand. Tell us what we are to do and we will do it." Out of this transformation, beginning from within, came projects of service and the penetration of a dechristianized society.[17]

In days when men everywhere cry out for the renewal of the church, it should be plain to all that such preaching of living doctrine is one essential source of new life. Groping men need a searching message of repentance through the power of the Holy Spirit. They need luminous teaching and persuasive call to growth into fuller maturity in the power of the Spirit. They need such instruction in the high meaning of life in the "body of Christ" as the Spirit of God can use to incorporate them into the serving unity of the people of God.

Letter from a King

Thus to preach New Testament doctrine is to deliver a message entrusted to us by Christ our King. In one of her essays, Isak Dinesen tells a story that aptly symbolizes the healing quality entrusted to such a ministry. On her vast farm in Africa, far from doctors and hospitals, she kept simple medications which she used to alleviate suffering for the people of the region. In the woods, one day, she came upon a man horribly crushed by a falling tree. Unable to treat so grave an injury, she and her workers loaded him into the car for the long trek to the nearest hospital. Caught without her

---

[17] From an address by Hendrik Kraemer at a meeting of the National Council of Churches of the U.S.A. held at Buck Hill Falls in 1957.

usual medicines to relieve his pain, she did what she could by way of suggestion, administering bits of sugar as if they were medicinal, until the small supply of even this makeshift was exhausted. As he begged, "Have you got nothing more to give me?" she rummaged in her pocket and came upon a letter.

It was a letter from the King of Denmark, written in his own hand, in appreciation of an unusually choice lion pelt she had sent in tribute. Bringing it out, she said to the injured man, "Yes, . . . I have got something more. I have got something . . . very excellent indeed. I have got a . . . letter from a king. And that is a thing which all people know . . . will do away with all pain, however bad." With this she laid the letter on the man's chest, putting her hand upon it. "I endeavored," she writes, "to lay the whole of my strength into it."

The effect was immediate, as if a healing power had gone all through him. His distorted features smoothed, his eyes closed. When he looked up again, it was to say in amazement, "It is very excellent indeed." Thus, all the way to the hospital and even on to the operating room, she held the letter which brought this balm.

The sequel spanned years that followed. For the news of the wonderful letter from the king spread over the countryside. No one ever asked for its special blessing for ordinary illnesses, but again and again, when suffering struck its worst blows or death loomed near, these people came to ask for its beneficent ministry. With the passing years it grew yellow, ragged, stained with blood, until it was no longer legible. But, the essay closes by saying:

The blood on my sheet of paper is not proud or edifying. It is the blood of a dumb nation. But then the handwriting on it is that of a king. . . . Within it, in paper and blood, a covenant has been signed between the Europeans and the Africans—no similar document of this same relationship is likely to be drawn up again.[18]

When we have done our best with our poor makeshifts of topical sermons and "inspiration" lifted out of texts taken piecemeal from here and there, the brokenness of men cries out to us, "Have you nothing more to give?" And we have a letter from a King, a message never so centered on its true essentials as when we focus on the basic doctrines of the apostolic preaching. Happy is the congregation whose minister, guided by the faithful teaching of these doctrines, can bring out the King's letter in all its reality and power. Twice happy if, with the tender strength and sure understanding of a pastor, he can lay it over men's hearts with the personal touch that meets their need.

Such a letter, in the hands of such a minister, has healing, life-giving power for our lost and menaced age. "Within it, in paper and blood, a covenant has been signed," between God and his people. "No similar document of this same relationship is likely to be drawn up again"—nor need be. Only men are needed who, sensing the treasure it contains, lay it healingly on broken lives.

FOR FURTHER STUDY

1. To the understanding of repentance and new life under the power of the Holy Spirit, John Wesley made contributions so

[18] *Shadows on the Grass* (New York: Random House, Inc., 1961), pp. 51-74.

lasting that preachers in all households of faith find the study of his work rewarding. His published *Sermons* are the most adequate way to encounter his doctrine, but for those who seek a briefer summary, *A Compend of Wesley's Theology*, edited by Robert W. Burtner and Robert E. Chiles (Nashville: Abingdon Press, 1954) is excellent. His tract, *A Plain Account of Christian Perfection*, is a classic which repays periodic rereading.

2. Sometime during the coming year, it will be helpful to prepare to "preach your way through" a major book of the Bible. Since Acts is supremely the book of the Holy Spirit, a careful exposition of its key passages would make such a preaching venture rewarding for both preacher and congregation.

If you have been carrying out the projects suggested along the way, you are developing a notebook opulent with resources for your planning of next year's preaching. It should make the final period of concentrated planning for the year a time of personal inspiration and joy in creation. In it you have established a beachhead for strong sallies into the new year's ministry. Congratulations! May God bless your continued progress.

Index of Scripture

Index of Names and Subjects